The Cardinal O'Hara Series
*Studies and Research in Christian Theology
at Notre Dame*

Volume III

The Cardinal O'Hara Series

STUDIES

AND RESEARCH

IN CHRISTIAN

THEOLOGY

AT NOTRE DAME

VOLUME THREE

PRESENT AND FUTURE

MODERN ASPECTS OF

NEW TESTAMENT THEOLOGY

Rudolf Schnackenburg

UNIVERSITY OF NOTRE DAME PRESS · 1966
NOTRE DAME · LONDON

NIHIL OBSTAT: Joseph Hoffman, C.S.C.,
  Censor Deputatus
IMPRIMATUR: ✠ Leo A. Pursley, D.D, L.L.D.,
  Bishop of Fort Wayne-South Bend

  May 16, 1966

Chapter VIII of this book appeared in its original form in
Die Johannesbriefe by R. Schnackenburg and Chapter IX
originally appeared in *Das Johannesevangelium* by
R. Schnackenburg. Both titles are published by Verlag Herder,
Freiburg, and will be published in an English edition by
Herder and Herder, New York.

PREFACE

This book was first delivered as a series of lectures at the University of Notre Dame in the fall of 1965. The gracious invitation of this university's department of theology gave me the opportunity to become acquainted with American academic life, to carry out many stimulating discussions, and to strengthen relations with biblical scholars and other theologians, both Catholic and Protestant, in the United States—an encouraging sign for the progress of the biblical movement and ecumenical dialogue. Besides a symposium to which two Protestant and two Catholic scholars contributed in a harmonious way and the lectures given at Notre Dame, I also lectured at other universities and colleges. Everywhere I found the same spirit of warmth and great hospitality. Therefore, I wish to express my sincere gratitude to all who invited and helped me: first of all to the Fathers of the Congregation of Holy Cross at Notre Dame and then, among all whom I cannot name, to Professor G. E. Ladd of Fuller Theological Seminary, who sponsored my lecture tour in southern California and who arranged things so conveniently for me.

Addressed primarily to students and then to a wider public, the lectures gathered here are intended to indicate the relevance of biblical theology for our present intellectual condition and our religious thought. The topics are randomly selected from the gospels and from Pauline and Johannine theology, and are assigned a title expressing approximately their main unifying feature. I have concurred with the wishes of the University of Notre Dame Press by preparing these essays for publication. For the translations I am indebted to Friar Denis Burkhard, O.F.M. Conv., and Mr. Michael Steinhauser, American students of theology at Innsbruck, Austria.

Rudolf Schnackenburg

Würzburg
January, 1966

CONTENTS

ABBREVIATIONS

Bib	*Biblica*, Rome
BZ	*Biblische Zeitschrift*, Neue Folge, Paderborn 1957 ff.
CBQ	*Catholic Biblical Quarterly*, Washington
LThK	*Lexikon für Theologie und Kirche*, 2nd rev. ed., 10 vol., Freiburg i.Br. 1957-65
NovT	*Novum Testamentum*, Leiden/Netherl.
RB	*Revue Biblique*, Jerusalem-Paris
ThWNT	*Theologisches Wörterbuch zum Neuen Testament*, 8 vol., Stuttgart 1933-66 (not yet completed)
ZNW	*Zeitschrift für die neutestamentliche Wissenschaft*, Berlin

Note. The biblical citations are taken, generally, from the Revised Standard Version (London and Glasgow: Collins Fontana Books). In a few cases only the text was slightly changed to correspond to the explanations given in the papers.

CHAPTER I

Present and Future in the Preaching of Jesus

Theology for a long time has overlooked the question of the meaning of history and the future of the human race—a sin of omission that is now beginning to avenge itself. This intellectual area, long neglected while we were engrossed in other aspects of our faith and its apologetics, is now being invaded by various intellectuals and ideologists. The Marxist philosophy of history, historical materialism, proclaims and strives toward a classless and stateless society that promises an earthly paradise to all men. This seductive, irreligious program misunderstands the nature of man and human history but responds to mankind's natural desire for happiness and peace. Yet, from its origin the Christian belief is a message touching humanity and the history of mankind, the good news of man's salvation. It proclaims the deliverance of our world from the powers of evil and the establishment of God's blessed rule.

1

Shaken by its existence in an atomic age and influenced by biblical theology and modern philosophy, present-day theology has seriously taken up the question of history and eschatology.[1] No other problem today is so passionately discussed as the existence and historicity of man. Therefore, we are prepared to hear and consider the eschatological message of Jesus.

In the area of biblical studies we are experiencing a new, disturbing interpretation of the eschatological message.[2] What is the original message of Jesus? What does it mean to call it eschatological? Would

[1] Selected bibliography: (Catholic) J. Daniélou, *Vom Geheimnis der Geschichte* (Stuttgart, 1956); H. Urs von Balthasar, *A Theology of History* (New York, 1963); R. A. F. McKenzie, S.J., *Faith and History in the Old Testament* (Minneapolis, 1963); R. Schnackenburg, *God's Rule and Kingdom* (New York, 1963); "*Mysterium Salutis*" (Grundrissheilsgeschichtlicher Dogmatik) eds. J. Feiner and M. Löhrer, vol 1, *Die Grundlagen heilsges*chichtlicher Dogmatik (Einsiedeln, 1965). (Protestant) R. G. Collingwood, *The Idea of History* (Oxford, 1946); A. N. Wilder, *Eschatology and Ethics in the Teaching of Jesus*, rev. ed. (New York, 1950); O. Cullmann, *Christ and Time* (Philadelphia, 1950) and *Heil als Geschichte* (Tübingen, 1965); W. Kamlah, *Christentum und Geschichtlichkeit*, 2nd. ed. (Stuttgart, Köln, 1951); G. E. Wright, *God Who Acts* (Naperville, 1952); K. Löwith, *Weltgeschichte und Heilsgeschehen* (Zürich, Wien, 1953); W. G. Kümmel, *Promise and Fulfilment* (Naperville, 1957); R. Bultmann, *History and Eschatology* (Edinburgh, 1955); E. C. Rust, *Salvation History* (Richmond, 1963) and *Towards a Theological Understanding of History* (New York, 1963); A. Richardson, *History Sacred and Profane* (London, 1964); W. Pannenberg, T. Rendtorff, and U. Wilckens, *Offenbarung als Geschichte* (Göttingen, 1961).

[2] For the history of research and a new evaluation cf. G. Lundström, *The Kingdom of God in the Teaching of Jesus* (Richmond, 1963); N. Perrin, *The Kingdom of God in the Teaching of Jesus* (Philadelphia, 1963); G. E. Ladd, *Jesus and the Kingdom, The Eschatology of Biblical Realism* (New York, 1964).

Jesus have announced apocalyptically the coming of the end of the world? Under this aspect would Jesus have called men to conversion and faith? Or are all his words that tell of the imminent coming of the kingdom of God only a form of expression conditioned by his time and bound to his environment? Did he actually wish to say and teach something about the future, or did he wish only to awaken men, to place them before the face of God, to urge them to a moral decision, to prepare them for radical obedience to the will of God? An influential school of thought[3] regards those statements about the future that foretell real events as nothing more than the mythological residue of an outdated view of the world. They further tend to demythologize the message of the primitive Christian community and to interpret it solely from our existential situation. This is a difficult question of hermeneutics, which is now coming under the influence of the so-called existential interpretation.[4]

First, we shall consider the future in the preaching of Jesus, especially whether it is an apocalyptic announcement or a mode of expression, an adaptation of the contemporary trend of thought and, therefore, really another message. Is it an eschatological event or, as one now expresses it, a "speech-event"? Second, we shall consider the present in the preaching of Jesus and its significance for his eschatological thought. Finally, we

[3] Namely, the school of R. Bultmann; for a representative viewpoint see N. Pervin, *Kingdom of God* 112-129.

[4] Cf. *The New Hermeneutic*, eds. James M. Robinson and John B. Cobb. Jr. (New York, 1964). In this volume, reflecting discussions among European and American theologians, see especially the most advanced view of Ernst Fuchs (Marburg).

shall examine the consequences of his message for the behavior and conduct of man, to whom the eschatological preaching of Jesus becomes a challenge.

I   THE FUTURE IN THE PREACHING OF JESUS

New trends in the field of exegesis deny Jesus' eschatological outlook. They transfer it to an apocalyptic movement in the early Church and consider this as the origin of all early Christian theology.[5] Therefore, we must ask whether the message of Jesus was in itself eschatologically accentuated: Does his message include the announcement of definite cosmic events such as the coming of the kingdom of God, the parousia of the Son of Man, the resurrection, and judgment? The discovery of the eschatological character of the preaching of Jesus has been a basic question in New Testament research since the turn of the century. It cannot be omitted in present biblical investigation for the following reasons.

1. According to the entire synoptic tradition—especially the parables, which are indisputably his original words—Jesus has proclaimed a message of the kingdom of God. It is undoubtedly an eschatological message, because the kingdom is of its essence eschatolo-

[5] For a discussion of various opinions in this direction see W. G. Kümmel, "Die Naherwartung in der Verkündigung Jesu," *Zeit und Geschichte, Dankesgabe an Rudolf Bultmann zum 80. Geburtstag* (Tübingen, 1964) 31-46. Kümmel himself holds a strong temporal outlook for the imminent future to be enclosed in Jesus' message of the kingdom of God. For another trend see also E. Käsemann, *Exegetische Versuche und Besinnungen*, vol. 2 (Göttingen, 1964) 82-104, 105-131.

gical. The parables of the kingdom—namely the figure of the banquet, the harvest, the mustard seed, the leaven, and others—are constantly directed to the coming of God's perfect kingdom. The sayings that deal with entering the kingdom of God, the beatitudes, the supplication "Thy kingdom come" in the *Our Father*, and, above all, the message that the kingdom of God is approaching (Mk 1:15) can only be explained as the announcement of God's kingdom, which is close at hand. This constitutes the central theme of the preaching of Jesus.

2. The probability of such a message in the preaching of Jesus is considerably increased by the situation and mentality of contemporary Judaism. It is a time bristling with messianism; men look especially to the future. They await a new kingdom, both political and spiritual, according to the individual conceptions they hold. This has been corroborated and confirmed by the Qumran texts. The Qumran community was deeply influenced by apocalyptic thoughts and essentially directed toward deliverance from this pernicious time.

3. Even if one cannot place Jesus within a clearly defined eschatological and apocalyptic school of thought, yet the consternation caused by his message among the people can only be explained by the fact that he stepped into a turbulent period with a definite eschatological message. This is best characterized as the "mystery of the kingdom of God" (Mk 4:11). The kingdom of God is coming: its full glory is still anticipated, but with the works of Jesus in the world it is present already in a certain manner. The kingdom powerfully presents itself: it is visible to all who have eyes to see.

The frequent references to the effectiveness of Jesus' works—God's mercy toward repentant sinners, expulsion of devils and healing of the sick, his announcement of the good news and his moral decisions—are intelligible only if they are signs of God's kingdom. The tension between the "here" and the "to-come" is already existent.

4. Certainly we cannot isolate the preaching of Jesus or categorize it as eschatological pronouncements of the imminent end of the world. What lies at the heart of his message is a new, immediate, and childlike relation of trust and fidelity to God, expressing itself in love of neighbor. This new man-God relation is essentially co-determined by the history of salvation and by the eschatological event that took place in Jesus. One could say that the eschatological element is an integrating moment of Christ's message, an indispensable viewpoint of his religious instruction, an irremovable motive for the commitment to his challenge.

5. Although it is being questioned at the present time, Jesus did speak certainly of the future parousia. The words "Every one who acknowledges me before men, the Son of Man also will acknowledge before the angels of God; but he who denies me before men will be denied before the angels of God" (Lk 12:8f.) hardly refer to early Christian prophecy, but rather veil a personal saying of Jesus that reveals his future coming in glory. Such masked expressions occur in many other passages, for example, the sign of Jonah (Lk 11:29f.) and the desolation of Jerusalem—"For I tell you, you will not see me again, until you say, 'Blessed

is he who comes in the name of the Lord' " (Mt 23:38f.). We recall, too, that Jesus before the Sanhedrin publicly confesses himself to be the exalted and awaited Son of Man (Mk 14:62), although the exact wording of his answer is perplexing. Also the eschatological discourse found in Mark 13, which in its present form is certainly a redaction of the Christian community, contains authentic sayings of Jesus, authorized by the early Christian Church. In addition to these important eschatological citations, there are lesser ones not to be overlooked, such as in Luke 17:22-37.

How to *interpret* Jesus' prophecies of the future is another question. The hypothesis of the so-called eschatologism, wherein Jesus announced the parousia and the advent of a perfect kingdom of God in the near future, is unjustified in its radical form. On the other hand, it is an undeniable fact that Jesus spoke to his contemporaries in a way that brought the judgment to them as an imminent event, as an occurrence that could befall anyone of them. Many Protestant scholars regard this as an error of Jesus and characterize it as irrelevant, since Jesus did not depend upon this temporal proximity of the end but upon its certainty and its consummation.[6] Just as the flower or the tree blossoms forth from the seed, so surely will God bring forth his kingdom, whose powers and

[6] A short note on the problem of how Jesus' expectation for the proximate future is to be understood is given in my article, "Naherwartung," *LThK* 7 (Freiburg, 1962) 777-779, with bibliography; see also A. Vögtle, "Exegetische Erwägungen über das Wissen und Selbstbewusstsein Jesu," *Gott in Welt, Festgabe für Karl Rahner*, vol. 1 (Freiburg, 1964) 608-677.

signs are already seen in the works of Jesus. Although
we do not admit an error of Jesus—nor did the
early Church—this conclusion is valid: the sayings of
Jesus point to a time that is approaching and yet they
do not specify when the end will come. This is clearly
expressed in Mark 13:32: "But of that day or that hour
no one knows, not even the angels in heaven, nor the
Son, but only the Father." Jesus wishes directly and
prophetically to challenge his hearers, just as the great
prophets of the Old Testament held before the eyes
of their contemporaries the imminent judgment of
God, in order that they might bring the children of
Israel back to him. Jesus, it seems, also makes use of a
prophetic form of preaching.

This will become clearer if we compare the preaching
of Jesus with the notions of the apocalyptic movement as they are known to us from all the literature
of the centuries before and after Christ. In the synoptic
gospels four typical *apocalyptic* questions are addressed to Jesus. His reaction to them is explicit. All
are found in the writings of Luke and reflect his proper
theological tendencies. Even if these are literary questions placed by Luke in the mouths of Jesus' listeners,
they nevertheless indicate certain conceptions prevalent at the time of Jesus. The gospel tradition reveals
Jesus' answer. The Pharisees ask Jesus when the kingdom of God is coming. And he answers, "The kingdom of God is not coming with signs to be observed;
nor will they say, 'Lo, here it is!' or 'There!' for behold,
the kingdom of God is in the midst of you" (Lk 17:20).
Jesus expressly refuses to specify the time when the
kingdom will come. Instead of designating an explicit

date, he refers his listeners to what has come to pass in their midst and demands their commitment. Luke gives us to understand three times in his two works that the disciples of Jesus were captivated by this feverish expectation of the kingdom of God (Lk 19:11, 24:21; Acts 1:6). But did Jesus give definite signs for the end? In the beginning of the great eschatological discourse his disciples ask, "Tell us, when will this be and what will be the sign when these things are all to be accomplished?" (Mk 13:4). That was the second apocalyptic question, and we would misunderstand Jesus if we thought the things that he named were genuine signs with which we could calculate the exact date of the parousia. Perhaps in the early Christian community there were groups who understood Jesus precisely in this manner, but his words themselves contain nothing that would give a positive temporal criterion for the end. If we consider the entire discourse, we see it is an admonition and consolation for the disciples in the afflictions, persecutions, temptations, and needs they must endure in this world. A third typical apocalyptic question appears in Luke 13:23: "Lord, will those who are saved be few? Jesus leaves his hearers in uncertainty about the number to be saved, but recalls to their mind the urgent admonition, "Strive to enter by the narrow door; for many, I tell you, will seek to enter and will not be able." One final question was important in apocalyptic circles of Jesus' time: "In which body will man arise? Speaking to the Sadducees (Mk 12:18-27), who denied the resurrection, Jesus answered that question by emphasizing the fact of the resurrection: "Is not this why you are wrong, that you

know neither the scriptures nor the power of God?"
Then he gives them scriptural proof that God will one
day raise the dead. But Jesus does not describe the
"how" of the resurrection or the type of body man
will have when he rises. Therefore, we conclude that
Jesus has dissociated himself from the form and mode
of thinking common in apocalyptic literature. He does
not desire to satisfy pious or impious curiosity but
seeks to make men maturely aware of what is to come.
The mystery of the "when" and "where" is reserved
to the knowledge and decision of God.

This fact gives us an important key to the understanding of Jesus' preaching about the future. The eschaton
is reserved to the wisdom and command of God. This
does not mean that we can know nothing about it.
Belief in events such as the resurrection and judgment
is found in most of the contemporary writers. Jesus
authoritatively defended this belief; above all, he proclaimed the salvific coming of the kingdom of God and
offered all men the possibility of entering it. He was
certainly concerned with the burning expectation of
salvation characteristic of his time. We might say that
he even placed himself in the apocalyptic movement.
Nevertheless, he amended the diverse notions concerning the future. The coming kingdom would not
find its fulfillment in the naturalistic anticipation of
a powerful earthly kingdom. He also dismissed the
apocalyptic calculations and their fantastic specula-
tions. It is not for men to know the time or the season
that the Father has determined by his own authority
(Acts 1:7). Luke's formulation retains the spirit of

Jesus. Also, all speculation about human relationships in the future kingdom of God is aimless (cf. Mk 12:25, 10:38f.). If Jesus, expressing himself in the contemporary mode, did not confine himself to its current notions, then surely he would not bind us to any special form of expression. Therefore, we are not bound to any ancient "mythological" idea of the world, which according to our present-day scientific knowledge is long obsolete. The revelation of Jesus justifies the endeavor of modern theology to overcome the naive concepts of the past.

An example of the Jewish notion of the resurrection will make this clear. First of all, man would rise with his old earthly body, with all his physical peculiarities, his weaknesses and idiosyncracies—and only by degree would he be transformed into a heavenly body (syr. Apocal. of Baruch 51). In the next world earthly relationships would in some form continue. Jesus thus addressed the Sadducees: "For when they shall rise from the dead, they neither marry, nor are given in marriage; but are as angels in heaven" (Mk 12:25).

Paul expresses it more clearly: "I tell you this, brethren, flesh and blood cannot inherit the kingdom of God, nor does the perishable inherit the imperishable. Lo, I tell you a mystery: We shall not all sleep, but we shall all be changed" (1 Cor 15:50f.). This means that, at the time of the resurrection, all men, both living and dead, will instantly be changed through the power of God into a new glorified body that will be completely different from our present earthly body. For all eschatological events we must keep before our eyes this transforming power of the new time, this mystery of God's new creation. Only in denying this would we contradict biblical revelation.

II THE PRESENT IN THE LIGHT OF THE ESCHATOLOGICAL PREACHING OF JESUS

We come to a full understanding of Jesus' preaching about the future only when we see it in its relation to the present. The actual message of Jesus does not touch the future but the present, in which he appears and preaches to men. "The time is fulfilled . . ." (Mk 1:15); "Today this scripture has been fulfilled in your ears," in that the captives are released, the blind see, the oppressed are freed, the acceptable year of the Lord is proclaimed (Is 61:1f.; Lk 4:18). Jesus also refers the messengers of John the Baptist to the blind who now see, the lame who walk, the lepers who are cleansed, the deaf who hear. To his disciples he proclaimed: "Blessed are the eyes which see the things that you see! For I tell you that many prophets and kings have desired to see what you see, and did not see it, and to hear what you hear, and did not hear it" (Lk 10:23f.). The present is, therefore, a moment of salvation in which the ancient prophecies approach fulfillment and in which the signs of world renewal, promised by God, come to light. The present is the beginning of the end, a time of God's grace. He has mercy on the misery of mankind, forgives sinners, and brings into his kingdom all men who turn to God and believe. This is the message of salvation, the gospel proclaimed by Jesus, which finds its fulfillment in his words and works. It is this that distinguishes his proclamation from all previous prophetic preaching. He not only promises the coming of salvation but also places it in the present, making its future fulfillment certain. If it is by the power of God that Jesus casts out demons, then the kingdom of God has come upon men (Lk 11:20). God has then established his kingdom, which is visible of course only to the eyes of believers. But nevertheless it is a reality filled with promise. This is the mystery of the kingdom of God that makes its first appearance in the works of Jesus. The external conditions of the world remain unchanged. Healings and miracles are still exceptions, but they are also signs that the powers of the world to come are already at work. Therefore, the present is both a time of fulfillment and a time of promise. It is a time of fulfillment for the promises that are now realized by God, and it is a time of promise for the glory still to come. A decisive change has actually occurred: salvation is offered to man—he needs only to grasp it. Of course, God does not dispense men from a free personal decision: they must turn from their former way of living, believe the gospel of God, accept the challenge preached by Jesus, and follow him. Therefore, the present is for them a time of decision, a crisis. Existential theologians affirm this truth. By his words and parables Jesus wishes to confront his contemporaries with the challenge and urgent appeal of God to convert and to believe. The parables of the unjust steward, the reference to the generation of Noah and the inhabitants of Sodom, the figures of the watchful servants and the virgins who await the bridegroom—all point out the significance of the present hour. This is the hour that demands readiness and haste. A decision made at this moment affects the future, while the same future places imperatives upon man here and now. The eschatological call of God bringing salvation to man, has here and now come through Jesus into this world. But man will reach the fullness of salvation only in the end, in the world to come.

Hence, the future regresses from the remote to the proximate and at the same time man's present is projected into the future. Let us consider what this means for the historical existence of man! Present-day philosophy tells us that each man through his personal decision in regard to the future chooses an area of action lying open before him. This sphere of possibility is determined and limited by his very decision. Placed in this situation each man proves himself to be a determiner of history. Only by accepting this and facing death as the end of personal decision, does man obtain a true human understanding of his existence. However, for the believer God has already determined the future: he need only decide for himself how he will participate in this future. If he commits himself to God in faith, he will be allotted the glory of God and will participate in the kingdom of God. But if he ignores the call of God and places himself over against God, he will also deprive himself of God's salvation. These things reveal the future to man, and yet they affect him as well as challenge him in the present. They are not simply doctrines, but words that concern man and touch him personally, compelling him to take a stand. No one has more deeply grasped the significance of Jesus' eschatological revelation than has John. That is the meaning of his "realized eschatology." "For God sent the Son into the world, not to condemn the world, but that the world might be saved through him. He who believes in him is not condemned; he who does not believe is condemned already, because he has not believed in the name of the only Son of God" (Jn 3:17f.). This present judgment, which the nonbeliever passes upon himself, does not deny the future judgment. But because this judgment is an irrevocable fact of the future, the present decision of the unbeliever becomes actual judgment. However, God does not desire judgment, but rather salvation; not death, but life. "He who believes in the Son, possesses eternal life"; he receives it already in the present from the Son, who has life in its fullness from the Father. This life is an eternal, indestructible divine life, whose glory will one day be revealed at the resurrection of the dead. John discloses the meaning of Jesus' eschatological preaching. It is not an apocalyptic revelation of a future event but a message of the saving action of God, which he works in the present and perfects in the future. The announcement of future events affirms the present salvation of men and reveals the message—the call and the challenge of God to all men. This is the meaning contained in the Sermon on the Mount that is directed to the present: it promises future salvation to men who are open to the gospel. "Blessed are you poor, for yours is the kingdom of God. Blessed are you who hunger now, for you shall be satisfied. Blessed are you who weep now, for you shall laugh" (Lk 6:20f.).

III THE NEED OF AN ESCHATOLOGICAL DISPOSITION

Some have called Jesus himself the eschatological event. Insofar as God leads the history of salvation to its summit by sending his Son, this title is justified. It would, of course, be a misconception if one wished to restrict the significance of Jesus to his very coming and his destiny as decided by God, namely, his crucifixion and resurrection. One cannot deny the significance of his words and doctrines. He had something relevant to say to humanity about the future and the present. Surely, the crucial revelation lies in the fact that God has raised the crucified Jesus from the dead. By this very act Christ himself is the meaning of history, the answer of God to all enigmatic questions of world events. The New Testament speaks often of the wisdom of God, of the great "mystery of Christ" that was hidden for all generations and has been revealed to us. The immediate meaning of this is not the revelation of this divine mystery as such but its significance for our salvation. This also seems to be the key to understanding Jesus' own words concerning the future and the present. If one attends to the proper meaning of Jesus' eschatological message, the tension between the "already" and the "not-yet" weakens and vanishes. His sayings do not emphasize the doctrine but rather the challenge and admonition. The prophetic style and form in which Jesus presents his preaching about the future manifests forcefully and solemnly that Jesus is concerned with the proper teaching of the eschatological disposition.[7]

Closer examination of Jesus' terminology on the future reveals definite eschatological virtues, which he continuously inculcated. First is the admonition to be *vigilant* and *ready*, which echoes through all his words and resounds in the apostolic preaching after Easter. The eschatological parables of the watchful servants who await the coming of their master, of the steward who guards his house, of the virgins who go to meet the bridegroom, time and again reveal this admonition. Certainly the primitive Christian community in its historical situation after Easter had revised such terms and applied them to their faithful. But we cannot doubt that they originally came from Jesus and that they constitute for his contemporaries an urgent appeal to men to prepare themselves for the approaching kingdom of God. The great eschatological discourse in Mark 13 ends in a threefold warning "Be watchful!" (33-37). Jesus' stand becomes a model; his advice to his disciples at Gethsemane, "Watch and pray that you may not enter into temptation!" (Mk 14:38), becomes the essence of the eschatological disposition demanded and presented by Christ.

Such readiness for the coming is far removed from any apocalyptic impatience and feverish anxiety. On the

[7] Cf. E. Neuhäusler, *Anspruch und Antwort Gottes* (Düsseldorf, 1962) 215-234; E. Lövestam, *Spiritual Wakefulness in the New Testament* (Lund, 1963); (to Luke:) W. Ott, *Gebet und Heil* (München, 1965).

contrary, in all eschatological watchfulness Jesus demands a grave calmness, since the end is undetermined
and cannot be calculated. His intense purpose is to bind
his disciples to the holy will of God and aid them to
trust in his decrees. The signs of horror before the end,
disaster and persecution, disunion and strife between
brothers, should not lead the disciples to despair. The
great eschatological discourse explains that "He who
endures to the end, will be saved" (Mk 13:13). Likewise Jesus says in another passage to "Fear not, little
flock, for it is your Father's good pleasure to give you
the kingdom" (Lk 12:32). The eschatological motive
develops into a theological one—commit yourselves intimately to the will of God, seek only his good pleasure and his grace! But since the powers of evil are
working in this world, *steadfastness, long-suffering,*
and patient *perseverance* are imperative. This great virtue that Paul proclaimed (the Greek ὑπομονή) is also
implicitly contained in Jesus' words on persecution and
death: "Whoever would save his life, will lose it; and
whoever loses his life for my sake, he will save it"
(Lk 9:24). To follow Jesus necessarily requires taking
up the cross, and Luke applies this to the daily life of
Christ's followers by inserting the word "daily" into
his words (Lk 9:23). When the burning hope of the
parousia was not immediately fulfilled, the early
Church emphasized and implanted this admonition.
But Jesus, the obedient servant of God, had already
presented this disposition in his suffering.

A genuine eschatological disposition is far removed
from that advocating flight from the world and a con-
tempt of the world—an attitude that leads to a neglect

of earthly tasks. True, the New Testament is not primarily concerned with temporal affairs, professional occupations, industrial organizations, and the like; nevertheless, work and vocation are not to be disregarded. In the foreground stands the apostolic mission. Conscious of its missionary work in the world, the early Christian community understood as a sign of that mission the parable of the servants to whom the master gave a definite task until he would return (Mt 25:14-30; Lk 19:12-27). Moreover, the pastors in the early Church understood in the same manner the parable of the steward whom his master set over his household (Mt 24:45-51; Lk 12:42-46). Luke in particular has vividly pictured this mission of Christ's disciples for the Church's temporal existence—meaning, of course, that we do not become "of the world," but that we go *into the world*. A certain reserve toward the world, a spirit of poverty toward seductive luxury, an inner detachment is always demanded. The Christian stands on guard—the Lord is always near; he can come at any time!

This, then, is the catalogue of eschatological virtues: vigilance and readiness, steadfastness and confidence, patient perseverance, as well as a sense of responsibility for the tasks imposed on us in this world. Luke has conclusively described for his readers the eschatological disposition of the Christian in the world. He formulates the words of Jesus at the end of the great eschatological discourse: "But take heed to yourselves lest your hearts be weighed down with dissipation and drunkenness and cares of this life, and that day come upon you suddenly like a snare; for it will come upon all who dwell upon the face of the whole earth. But watch at all times, praying, that you may have strength to escape all these things that will take place, and to stand before the Son of Man" (Lk 21:34-36). In a similar way, aware of our tasks in the midst of the modern world and of our mission in this world, we should adhere to what Jesus intended in his eschatological preaching, and in his spirit we should apply it to our proper historical situation.

CHAPTER II

The Challenge of the
Sermon on the Mount

Today's avid interest in and intense probing of Jesus' moral directives are indeed significant indications of the condition of contemporary Christianity. The shock of both world wars, sociological upheavals, a stronger awakening to social consciousness, the pressing search in philosophy and literature for the meaning of human existence, along with many other new developments, seem to leave very little room for a middle-class morality that hides its lack of Christianity behind the mask of a Christian appearance. Much in this morality was worthless and decrepit, amounting merely to external trimmings and face value. It would be unwise to claim that our present age, because of its social institutions, surpasses that prior to World War I. We need only to recall the problems of sexual morality, marriage, and family stability to dispel this illusion. But in the course of revolutionary changes in our way of life, the former Christian middle-class complacency and hypocrisy are now being outlawed. A Christian is now more likely to be disturbed by the incongruity between the law of Christ and his own way of life that he seems to regard as Christian. In this chapter I direct my considerations to those who seriously search for the meaning of Christianity; to older Christians who feel themselves oppressed, even crushed, by the demands of Christian moral teaching; and to younger Christians who want to structure their life according to Christ's directives but still experience weakness in their own flesh and an almost insuperable opposition proposed by the modern world.

Jesus' Sermon on the Mount proposes an acute and urgent challenge. We dare not insincerely tone down Jesus' words, cowardly push them aside, or evade what they demand of us.[1] Christ's words challenge us to an honest answer. Is it at all possible for us to realize these extreme demands? We believe that Jesus is God's definitive ambassador, who has proclaimed the undis-

[1] Selected bibliography: (Catholic) Th. Soiron, *Die Bergpredigt Jesu* (Freiburg, 1941); J. Dupont, *Les Béatitudes* (Bruges, Louvain, 1954), 2nd rev. ed., vol. 1, *Le problème litteraire* (1958); E. Neuhäusler, *Anspruch und Antwort Gottes* (Düsseldorf, 1962) 141-169; H. Kahlefeld, *Der Jünger. Eine Auslegung der Rede Lk 6,20-49* (Frankfurt a. M., 1962); R. Schnackenburg, *The Moral Teaching of the New Testament* (New York, 1965) 54-89. (Protestant) H. Windisch, *Der Sinn der Bergpredigt*, 2nd ed. (Leipzig, 1937); M. Dibelius, *The Sermon on the Mount*, Shaffer Lectures, Yale University, 1937 (New York, 1940); A. N. Wilder, *Eschatology and Ethics in the Teaching of Jesus*, rev. ed. (New York, 1950); A. M. Hunter, *Design for Life, An Exposition of the Sermon on the Mount* (London, 1953); P. Bonnard, *Le Sermon sur la Montagne*, (Neuchâtel, Paris, 1956); W. D. Davies, *The Setting of the Sermon on the Mount* (New York, 1964).

guised and unabridged truth and the will of God. But if we read his Sermon on the Mount in its stark reality, we are terrified: Can we truly be Christians, disciples of Christ? Not wanting to oversimplify the answer, we shall first consider a few of the inadequate solutions; then we shall attempt a fundamental reply taken from the totality of Jesus' preaching and from the tenor and basic concern of his message; finally, we must face the difficult task of deciding upon some concrete directives for our present Christian existence.

I   INSUFFICIENT ANSWERS

It is always valuable for the Christian exegete to familiarize himself with the exegesis of Jewish scholars because of their natural proximity to Jewish thought. Jesus as a Jew was well versed in Scripture; he disputed with the scribes and drew upon it (namely, the Old Testament) for his proofs although, of course, in a way that was new and stimulating. "He was teaching them as one having [divine] authority, and not as the scribes," remarks Mark 1:22. How, then, do modern Jewish scholars respond to the Sermon on the Mount? Into their writings is woven the opinion that the rigorism of Jesus' demands creates the impression of a highly moral and religious aspiration, but that this rigorism is a moral hindrance and foreign to life. The Torah, or Jewish law, should enforce the will of God on Israel, thus permeating the world and giving it form. But the exaggerated rigorism of Jesus makes this impossible and has a harmful effect. A few excerpts from J. Klausner's book, *Jesus of Nazareth*, make this clear:

Judaism also knows the ideal of love for the enemy, and exemplifies it in the law dealing with an enemy's ox or ass and in the ethical teaching of the Book of Jonah; but Judaism never emphasized it to such a degree that it ultimately became too high an ideal for ordinary mankind, and even too high for the man of more than average moral calibre. And the same applies to the ideal of "turning the other cheek." Judaism also praised them "who when affronted affront not again," but it never emphasized the idea unduly, for it would be difficult for human society to exist with such a basic principle. Judaism did not forbid swearing and litigation, but enjoined "a righteous yea or nay" and, in the person of Hillel, laid down the principle, "Judge not thy neighbour till thou art come into his place." Everything which Jesus ever uttered of this nature is Jewish ethical teaching, too; but his overemphasis was not Judaism, and, in fact, brought about non-Judaism."[2]

H. J. Schoeps, another Jewish scholar, thinks that the Sermon on the Mount by no means intended to give commandments for this world, but intended to describe the conditions for the perfect, future world.

Jesus believed, in accordance with the customary Jewish expectation of time, that the great turning-point of the ages was impending and in so far as he had a secret knowledge of himself as the awaited Messiah and Son of man, he might and indeed he must make clear in his beatitudes and antitheses the nature of this turning-point. The Sermon on the Mount is not connected with just any sort of ethical inquiry; it does not allow us to gain one single positive aspect in judging its position with regard to the Jewish law. We can, however, indirectly maintain that when the kingdom should arrive, along with this age the Jewish law would

[2] J. Klausner, *Jesus of Nazareth, His Life, Times, and Teaching,* 3rd ed. (London, 1947) 392.

itself "cease"—since it would be superseded. Actually, it would then be possible to fulfil it in its most radical sense, because then there will exist a harmony between what a person should do and what he can do, between the law and our acts, between God's will and man's wishes."[3]

Unfortunately, this well-disposed interpretation is untenable, because obviously the conditions of this world would then be presupposed for the future kingdom of God as proclaimed by Jesus. But according to Jesus' preaching, in the future world there will no longer be law suits, or marriage, or hostilities. From the interpretation of these Jewish scholars it would seem an impossibility to the Jewish mentality that Jesus' demands could be realized in *this* world. We admit in all honesty that most men of today sense the very same thing.

Among Protestant exegetes we find not a few who would make a virtue of necessity. They concede that Jesus' demands in the Sermon on the Mount are objectively unattainable; but they add that Jesus consciously raised his demands so as to prepare men to understand that they are not saved by their own initiative, that is, by observing every prescript of the law, but that they are saved only by God's grace. Man would be a sinner and remain one, were it not for Jesus' redeeming blood. This was formerly a frequent interpretation of the Sermon on the Mount. H. Windisch, however, reminded exegetes of their obligation to interpret the Sermon on the Mount not subsequent to Pauline thought, but for what it contains in itself.[4] We find nothing here about man's total inability to ful-

[3] "Jesus und das jüdische Gesetz," *Aus frühchristlicher Zeit* (Tübingen, 1950) 212-220, especially 214.
[4] See H. Windisch, *Der Sinn der Bergpredigt*.

fill these commands. Anyone who without prejudice allows Jesus' demands to take course cannot deny that Jesus surely wanted men to commit themselves to the actual observance of them.

Consequently, many exegetes today oppose any interpretation of liberal theology which maintains that moral observance is entirely a matter of one's intention and, further, that the Sermon on the Mount remains, both in its details and its essentials, bound to its environment and so cannot be reconciled with our present culture.

Above every detail stands the entirely unique purity, spirituality, and sensitivity of one's disposition, which is what we call ethos in its most profound sense. There exists no literary witness for such a closed characterization, for such powers of self-inversion. There is no need of higher academic training for it to exhibit a sensitivity and a profundity expressed in symbolic language and a sweeping view of the world of nature and spirit.[5]

When we read statements like this from the year 1921, we experience a certain contrast which our sense of life has gleaned from so humanitarian a mode of thought, but also—despite all its superlatives—the feebleness and insufficiency of its judgment of Jesus. Was he, after all, only a man with an unsurpassable sensitivity for a pure morality and an interior piety? Did he not perhaps have other aims?

Rudolf Bultmann's book about Jesus, which first appeared in 1926, was like a cleansing rainfall. Bultmann speaks of the radical obedience demanded by Christ,

[5] O. Baumgarten, *Bibel und Kultur der Gengenwart* (Tübingen, 1921) 117.

an obedience that compels every man here and now faced with an existential moment of decision. He protests precisely against the interpretation we mentioned a moment ago. Bultmann writes:

We cannot follow *that* solution, which maintains that it is entirely a matter of one's intention and which separates the intention from the act, seeing in the act an ideal way of acting which will perhaps at some future time be realized if man only keeps his good intention alive and if he continues to educate himself. . . . [Jesus] sees a definite person at the very moment of decision, and the decision is not something relative, but absolute. . . . The demands of the Sermon on the Mount, therefore, do not represent a moral idealism, but highlight the absolute character of God's demands![6]

In the above words, Jesus' challenges have been categorically placed before us. As we examine Bultmann's further conclusions we recognize a modern existential theology that is capable of addressing and stimulating the man of today—but one that we could scarcely prove to be the mind of Christ. Bultmann thinks that Jesus in no way proposes to men any demands whose meaning is fixed, but merely wants to bring men nearer to God's demand, which is in itself quite recognizable.

Whatever God's will is, it is not imposed by any external authority, so that the meaning of what is commanded would be equally valid, but it is confided to men and ex-

[6] R. Bultmann, *Jesus* (Tübingen, 1926, 1951) 81f; American ed. *Jesus and the Word* (New York, 1934). The references are taken from the German original. Cf. also the modified view of his pupil G. Bornkamm, *Jesus von Nazareth* (Stuttgart, 1956) 92-100, 201-204; American ed. *Jesus of Nazareth* (New York, 1960).

pected that they themselves will discover what is asked of them. God's demands are, therefore, recognizable. At the same time the concept of obedience is at first radically thought out.[7]

God's demands, he says, "quite simply grow out of a situation, in which man finds himself, where he must decide before God." No, Jesus claims an authoritative knowledge of God's will ("But I say to you . . ."), which contains specific demands. It has always been the interpretation of the Church, upon the testimony of the apostolic Fathers as early as the second century, that Jesus' demands in relation to the Old Testament law introduced innovations and that Christ's law must be fulfilled by acts.

Perhaps these brief considerations of the later interpretations have brought us to a better understanding of how difficult and weighty the question of fulfilling the law is. Perhaps Catholic moral theology has not always escaped the danger of toning down Jesus' radical demands in order to make them appear more reasonable. The opinion of some moral theologians, that Jesus' moral teaching is fundamentally no more than an interpretation of the natural law and a Christian statement of it, hardly does justice to Jesus' message. The disparity existing between a purely natural ethics and Christian morality is certainly greater.[8] An ethics proceeding from the nature of man and treating only a

[7] R. Bultmann, *Jesus* 68.

[8] Cf. R. Schnackenburg, "Die neutestamentliche Sittenlehre in ihrer Eigenart im Vergleich zu einer natürlichen Ethik," *Moraltheologie und Bibel* (Paderborn, 1964) 39-69; E. Hamel, *Loi naturelle et loi du Christ* (Bruges, Paris, 1964)—more traditionally.

natural man can never justify Jesus' challenging and astounding demands set forth in his Sermon on the Mount. In order to obtain a true and valid answer as to how we are to understand Jesus' unique moral message, we must turn our attention to the totality of Jesus' preaching.

II JESUS' DEMANDS IN THE FRAMEWORK OF HIS MESSAGE

Jesus brought a religious message that Mark has strikingly summarized at the moment when Jesus began his public ministry: "The time is fulfilled, and the kingdom of God is at hand. Repent and believe in the gospel" (1:15). Jesus is saying in fact that with his appearance the promises of the prophets concerning the consummation of the days are fulfilled, and that the final days of salvation have begun. For this reason his preaching is also called eschatological, that is, a preaching concerned with these final realities. Jesus takes this representation from the second part of the Book of Isaiah: God comes along a broad royal highway in order to establish his plenary rule. A messenger of good will precedes him and carries his good news to Jerusalem, as is found in Isaiah 52:7: "How beautiful upon the mountains are the feet of him who brings good news and who proclaims peace; of him who shows forth goodness, who preaches salvation, who says to Zion: Your God shall rule." The different expressions, such as peace, goodness, salvation, all suggest the same thing: that definitive salvation which God bestows upon man, when he seizes possession of his power as

king. That is the *Eu-angelion* or the good news from
God that he will now redeem a hopeless mankind.

The characteristic note of Jesus' eschatological preaching is found in the fact that salvation begins to be realized with his very coming, in his person and work, although it has not yet attained its perfection. God's
kingly rule makes its entry with him and proclaims itself in signs of grace: in his forgiving of sins, healing
the sick, casting out devils. But God's perfect rule, the
kingdom of God, still remains a future reality. Jesus
promises that it is a great, almost imminent event
whereby evil will be effectively wiped out, the glory of
God will shine throughout the whole world, and the
fullness of salvation will be bestowed upon the good.
Thus, Jesus' message becomes God's final offer of salvation to mankind: Be converted and believe in the
good news! The point of departure for Jesus' moral imperative lies precisely in this preaching of the kingdom.[9] Because God's salvific rule is a present reality,
salvation is not only a promise or future expectation
but is at this very moment a possibility for those who
convert and believe. With Jesus begins, to employ a
phrase from his sermon in Nazareth, the "acceptable

[9] Cf. R. Schnackenburg, *Moral Teaching*, chap. 1, and *God's
Rule and Kingdom* (New York, 1963) 104-113. Recently, more
stress has been laid upon the immediate relationship of man to
God, which Jesus had taught within the framework of his
message of God's kingdom. Cf. E. Neuhäusler, *Anspruch und
Antwort Gottes*; H. Schürmann, "Das hermeneutische Haupt-
problem der Verkündigung Jesu," *Gott in Welt*, *Festgabe für
Karl Rahner* vol. 1 (Freiburg, 1964) 579-607. But I doubt that
we should be allowed to obscure the fact of Jesus' definite
eschatological message even though the other aspect is also
included in it.

year of the Lord" (Lk 4:19). But since God has not yet bestowed the fullness of salvation to the whole of mankind, it remains an offer that every hearer of the gospel must accept and realize for himself. If he is obedient to God's will and observes his demands as proclaimed by Jesus, he can "enter the kingdom of God" (cf. Mt 7:21) and participate in the future reign of glory.

We must now consider the position of the Sermon on the Mount in the totality of Jesus' preaching. The beatitudes at the very beginning are no more than the assurance of the full reality of salvation for whoever is prepared and responsive to them. "Blessed are the poor in spirit, for theirs is the kingdom of heaven. . . ." Then Jesus constantly employs new images for the same salvation, which is the blessing of God's rule. "They shall be comforted, they shall inherit the earth, they shall be satisfied, shall obtain mercy, shall see God, shall be called sons of God," and finally once again "Blessed are those who are persecuted for righteousness' sake, for theirs is the kingdom of heaven." (Mt 5:3-10). It also made clear that certain prerequisites are necessary on the part of men, at least in the version of Matthew. The Evangelist understands that all to whom salvation is announced, the poor, those who mourn, the meek, must also have the corresponding moral disposition. But this is basically the attitude of Jesus himself. Under the image of entering into the kingdom of God, Jesus' demands of the applicant are lofty and difficult. "Unless your justice exceeds that of the scribes and Pharisees, you shall not enter the kingdom of heaven" (Mt 5:20) and "Enter by the narrow gate" (7:13). Luke writes even more pointedly: "Strive to enter by the narrow gate; for many, I tell you, will seek to enter and will not be able" (13:24). Both evangelists hand on the significant saying: "Seek first the kingdom of God, and all else will be given you besides" (Lk 12:31; cf. Mt 6:33). These words give us the key to an understanding of the Sermon on the Mount: it is a powerful appeal to all who await the kingdom of God and who strive for it. Now we understand why Jesus hardly ever takes into account earthly conditions. With unconcerned one-sidedness he proclaims the absolute and holy will of God and challenges men with a most important and burning task, proposed to them at this salvation-laden hour.

Yes, at this hour. Not, however, as computed by man. The hour of salvation is Jesus' presence. From the note of urgency in Jesus' message, namely, that God's rule has approached, and from the expressions stressing its nearness, we should like to conclude that he awaits in the proximate future the final events of the cosmos. This is the thesis of eschatologism, according to which Jesus was mistaken about the exact time of the end.[10] We cannot go into particulars here, but there do exist other texts that are opposed to this interpretation and leave all chronological indication of the end undetermined except in the Father's knowledge (Mk 13:32; Lk 17:20).

Nothing should disturb us if we comprehend the full tenor of Jesus' preaching, which carries with it a pro-

[10] This is the thesis of A. Schweitzer, M. Werner, and others; cf. for information and discussion H. Schuster, "Die konsequente Eschatologie in der Interpretation des Neuen Testaments, kritisch betrachtet," *ZNW* 47 (1956) 1-25; F. J. Schierse, "Eschatologismus," *LThK* 3 (1959) 1098f.

phetic urgency and calls mankind to a decision. We must free ourselves from preoccupation with time and learn to think biblically, in the context of the history of salvation. Jesus has definitively and irrevocably brought salvation to us—though charged with inner consequences for us. Only at the end will God's dynamic salvific rule become his perfect glorious kingdom, and only if we prove true and persevere shall we participate in it. The parables describing the growth of grain illustrate this. The seed might not be visible but it has been planted, and with certainty it moves toward the harvest once it has been summoned forth by God's will and power (Mk 4:26-29). We may wait calmly and trustfully for the coming harvest but, on the other hand, we can forfeit our salvation if we disregard the demands of God implied in this salvific message. This is the meaning of the explanation the Christian community has added to the parable of the sower (Mk 4:13-20), applying the parable to its own situation.

The ethics of the New Testament assumes its true character only when seen from this eschatological point of view. It is not an ethics of some interim period, that is, an emergency moral theology intended just for the short interval until the end, and in which all earthly realities would be totally incidental and unimportant. It is an eschatological ethics insofar as all earthly realities attain a character of temporality, of inconstancy, of feebleness. Moreover, in this current age of as yet unrealized salvation, in which we Christians nevertheless already belong to the future kingdom of God, there is but one care: to attend to the things of God (Mt 6:24), to love God with all our heart and with all our

soul and with all our mind (Mt 22:37). At the moment
when God's rule appears, his will should be exhibited
to Jesus' disciples in all its purity and perfection, and it
should become for them the exclusive norm of their
lives. The consequences this might entail for them are
depicted by Jesus (and the evangelists, respectively) in
his Sermon on the Mount employing images and parables taken from the circumstances of life peculiar to
his times. Indeed, a more radical or a more rigorous line
of thought appears in Jesus' speech. But before going
any further into the problem of observance, we should
clarify something else in Jesus' eschatological preaching. Why should Jesus be the first to declare God's will
so absolutely? Because through him man first became
capable of perceiving and obeying God's absolute will
of holiness. Jesus does not simply appear before men as
a new lawgiver, but simultaneously and primarily as
the bearer of God's salvation. Only because he com-
municates to men God's love and salvation, can he and
does he will to communicate to them God's lofty demands as well. Otherwise how could he affirm, on the
one hand, "I have not come to call the just, but sinners" (Mk 2:17), while on the other hand he says that
only he who does the will of his Father in heaven will
enter the kingdom of God? How could he maintain that
his yoke is sweet and his burden light (Mt 11:30), and
in the same breath demand the almost inhuman? This
apparent contradiction is resolved when we consider
that he proclaims to men the inconceivable greatness
of God's love, his unlimited readiness to forgive, and
that the consequence of his proclamation is to summon
men to a more noble, more grateful mutual love (cf. Mt

18:23-35; Lk 19:1-10). He receives in God's name the despised tax collectors and prostitutes, but likewise instructs them not to sin again (Mk 2:15-17; Lk 7:36-50). *God demands much because he gives much; he requires great things because he imparts and promises still greater blessings.*

Finally, we have yet to consider one other point. For those who awaited God's kingdom and who heard the Sermon on the Mount, Jesus' summons to undivided service of God meant at the same time an appeal to enter the ranks of his disciples, to follow him. They should experience concretely in his constant discipleship how they should have ordered and shaped their life.[11] To a certain extent the Sermon on the Mount is a general program which is to be further specified for every individual by personal contact with Jesus. As far as we can determine, Jesus also dealt with his disciples as individuals. From one he demanded complete renunciation of his worldly possessions, for instance, from the rich young man (Mk 10:21), whereas from another he did not demand this, as with Zacchaeus, the head tax collector (Lk 19:1-10). One he would leave to his earthly affairs, another he would admit among his immediate companions and helpers with his work. Not that the fundamental demands of the Sermon on the

[11] For the notion of "discipleship" see K. H. Schelkle, *Jüngerschaft und Apostelamt*, 2nd ed. (Freiburg, 1961), or American ed. *Discipleship and Priesthood* (New York, 1965); A. Schulz, *Nachfolgen und Nachahmen* (München, 1962); E. Schweizer, *Erniedrigung und Erhöhung bei Jesus und seinen Nachfolgern*, rev. ed. (Zürich, 1962) 7-21; H. Zimmermann," "Christus nachfolgen," *Theologie und Glaube* 53 (1963) 241-255; R. Schnackenburg, *Moral Teaching* 42-53.

Mount were lessened by the concrete following of Jesus—quite the contrary! When he later manifested the mystery of his passion and death to his closest disciples, he demanded an imitation of his sacrifice upon the cross and the surrender of their lives on his behalf (Mk 8:34). Many things became clearer to the disciples as they continued to view the Master and his conduct. They learned that to turn one's cheek does not signify a weak softness of character: from Jesus' discourses calling for battle against the unbelieving leaders of the people, the disciples learned that they must courageously and steadfastly defend God's rights. To love one's enemy does not mean a cowardly, defenseless humbling of oneself (cf. Jn 18:22f.), but it does mean praying for those who hate and murder (Lk 6:27f., 23:34). In short, Jesus' acts clarify his words —a principle of which the Fathers of the Church were well aware.

We are now in a position to judge the language Jesus used in the Sermon on the Mount. Without wanting to lessen in the least the weight of his words, we must nevertheless observe that in accordance with the pedagogy of his times Jesus used images and examples that we would misunderstand were we to take them literally. To express the idea that we should not retaliate, he uses three images: "If a man strikes you on the right cheek, turn the other cheek also toward him; if he is ready to go to law with you over your coat, let him have it and your cloak as well; if anyone forces you to go one mile, go two miles with him" (Mt 5:39ff.). Jesus means by these exaggerated images to clarify his admonition. They are, however, only pictures, so that in the example of the lawsuit Jesus obviously did not intend to dismiss the whole process of law. Again, should we seriously believe that Jesus allowed only prayer in the privacy of one's room, or that he completely ruled out public almsgiving, or recommended to those who fast the practice of rubbing themselves down with oil (Mt 6:1-18)? That is figurative language from which we must draw the lesson he intended.

This conclusion represents the explanation of several problems. In the discourse about divorce, which the synoptic writers expressly hand down to us, Jesus clearly and in God's name forbade this practice, although it had formerly been Jewish policy (Mk 10:1-9; cf. Mt 5:31f.). Is that also the case regarding his prohibition of swearing, which is found only in the Sermon on the Mount (Mt 5:33-36)? Or did he only intend to correct the private abuse of swearing, which was at that time a widespread bad habit in Judaism? Such problems cannot be solved exegetically with certitude. When interpreting Jesus' figurative language, we must not destroy the lesson he had in mind; nor may we set aside his examples. We must try to penetrate Jesus' more profound intention as expressed in this language. Then we must apply his directives to our particular circumstances of life and to our own personal situation. This will lead us to the third part of our considerations, that is, how to apply the demands of Jesus' Sermon on the Mount to our present Christian existence, without diminishing their force, and at the same time fulfilling them without becoming religious fanatics.

III   JESUS' DEMANDS APPLIED TO OUR TIME
AND CIRCUMSTANCES

The evangelists in a certain way seemed to have imposed this task upon us. Matthew arranged the Sermon on the Mount for his Judaeo-Christian readers, whereas Luke did so for a pagan-Christian public. The third evangelist, for example, while remaining faithful to the spirit of Jesus, omitted several things that were incomprehensible and unsuitable for the earlier pagans. With unheard of trenchancy he centers attention on what is most important—the commandment of love. After the beatitudes and the "woes," he immediately takes up the theme of love for our enemies and demonstrates with Jesus' words exactly how far our love for our fellowmen must go if we are to imitate the paradoxical love of God for us. He formulates in another version the words passed down by Matthew, "But love your enemies, and do good, and lend, not hoping for any return, and your reward shall be great, and you shall be children of the Most High, for he is kind toward the ungrateful and evil" (Lk 6:35). Therefore, it is obvious that by love of enemies is meant love for those contemporaries who deserve our love, with whom, according to our natural human inclination, we do not want to have any part but who nevertheless need our help. God's challenge comes to us through them. How we help them, be it by a personal act or by material assistance, by a generous gift or a loan without charging interest, or whatever it might be, depends entirely on our circumstances, as long as we hear God's challenge and imitate his example. God loves us although we are not deserving of his love; he pardons our sins although they offend and provoke him; and our ingratitude he overlooks. Fundamentally, loving our enemies is only one definite form of love for our neighbor. In the classical example of the good Samaritan, it is a Jew who in the course of a journey has been wounded and who is a stranger and even a national enemy to his benefactor (Lk 10:30-37). Hidden in the love that Jesus, in imitation of God, demands of us, lies the germ of selfless, self-conquering love. In the final analysis this is how we must understand the twofold commandment of love of God and neighbor. The words "Love your neighbor as yourself" should set no boundaries to our love for our fellow men, but should point out that whatever we do for ourselves, we should do also for our neighbor. There is no hesitation here, because each knows spontaneously what is asked of him.

What we have thus far learned is an extremely important, even decisive, principle for the practical application of Jesus' demands. It is a principle that assuredly corresponds to the spirit of Jesus. *All the demands of the Sermon on the Mount are summed up in the most important commandment—to love.* Its double form, in which both love of God and neighbor are equally important, becomes an immediate norm of our conduct. Genuine love of God proves itself in love of neighbor even to the point of loving our enemies. In return, in the love of our brothers we are certain of our love for God. For anyone who reflects upon Jesus' notions of love, the demands of the Sermon on the Mount become clear and transparent, simple and yet in every situation new. Whoever truly loves God knows what God wants of him here and now. Herein lies the truth of St. Augustine's words "Love and do what you will." An audacious saying that can be easily abused, but for anyone who truly loves it becomes a golden key. Naturally, when we scan the broad field of moral theology and consider the complicated situations of life, many individual questions remain—all of which we cannot treat. But we should be mindful of some crucial points in Jesus' moral instructions, of things that obviously interested him deeply and that reveal his closeness to life and knowledge of men. Jesus showed wealth to be one of the most dangerous temptations. Jesus' saying about serving two masters is significant: "You cannot serve God and mammon" (Mt 6:24; Lk 16:13). Another characteristic admonition is "Do not lay up for yourselves treasures on earth . . . but lay up for yourselves treasures in heaven . . . for where your treasure is, there will your heart be also" (Mt 6:19-21; Lk 12:33f.). Fundamentally, every disciple is called to renounce his earthly possessions on behalf of Jesus. We have, however, seen earlier that the summons is concretely different for each individual. In our self-examinations we might ask: How do I use earthly goods? What does God want of me?

Furthermore, Jesus thinks pessimistically about our struggling for acceptance. In the Sermon on the Mount he lashes out against the superficial piety of certain groups of Pharisees who act only "that they might be seen by men" (Mt 6:1, 5, 16). He later warned even his own disciples about this striving for power. Whoever would consider Jesus to be Utopian, ignorant of the world, need only once reflect upon his realistic judgment: "You know that those who claim to be rulers about the Gentiles lord it over them, and their great men exercise an authority over them. But it is not so among you. On the contrary, whoever wishes to become great shall be your servant; and whoever wishes to be first among you shall be the slave of all" (Mk 10:42f.). Once again such words must be explained in accordance with Jesus' intention; by no means did he wish to condemn all rulers. He did not reject either Nicodemus, a leader in the community, or Joseph of Arimathea, an influential citizen. But he did condemn most severely the love of power and branded it as incompatible with the discipleship to which he called them. The early Church, too, had its leaders, and we are well aware that this saying of Jesus was a constant reminder for them. Luke transfers the incident of the apostles' dispute over precedence, and Jesus' answer, to the Last Supper (Lk 22:24-27)—obviously a reference to the leaders of the community who exercise their duty of brotherly service precisely when the community comes together for this holy meal. In this way the early Christian tradition applied Jesus' sayings and directives to the situation of the early Church and interpreted them in terms of her life. This task is also ours and no one can refuse it. The Church does this only to a certain extent when she tries to determine concretely the implications of Jesus' demands in our present circumstances. But in addition each one of us must reflect upon his own situation and personal obligations and thus constantly bear the weight and judgment of the Lord's words in his Sermon on the Mount.

To mention one other area, one which causes great difficulties for us, let us briefly consider Jesus' position with regard to sexuality. It is rather strange that he does not warn us more often and more forcefully about the destructive potentialities of this instinct that in itself is willed by God. Its gripping power was no less forceful in Jesus' time than it is today. But to Jesus it was not the number one enemy of man's salvation: frequently he experienced the genuine sorrow and conversion of those who sinned through weakness and recognized that in such cases there is a better starting point for God's grace than in those who are hardened in their pride and whose love is dead. Jesus condemned unrestricted lust as well as sins of action (Mt 5:27-30), and in the question of divorce he assumed an unyielding position (Mt 5:31f.), but he loved penitent sinners and prostitutes and granted God's forgiveness to them. This final point suggests once again the problem of fulfilling Jesus' demands. How encouraging is Jesus' reply—now revealed to us not so much by any explicit saying but more by his entire conduct. Despite our existence in the new order of salvation, we are as men tempted and discouraged by our weakness. We are tempted to say that Jesus' demands cannot be observed, but such thoughts are a form of temptation. Jesus' reply to us today is the same as that given to his disciples: "With men it is impossible, but not with God" (Mk 10:27).

In conclusion, let us recall that God's mercy does not cease for Christ's weak disciples. We must not subtract anything from the holiness and rigorism of Christ's demand, but must again and again be personally challenged by them in each unique and novel situation. We must live the conviction of our faith that we are hidden in God's love, who wills only our salvation. He is the same God who demands lofty moral activity of us and who loves us in his Son and preserves us until the day of our full redemption.

CHAPTER III

Miracles in the New Testament and Modern Science

In the Old and New Testaments we find many dramatic stories concerning miraculous events. These present us with a concept of miracle and various aspects of miraculous event that appear disconsonant with modern scientific thinking. In this chapter an attempt will be made to compare and contrast the mode of thinking in the Bible with that of the contemporary scientific world. One can hardly begin by defining "miracle," for the ancient and the modern mind think in different dimensions. In the first part of this chapter we shall try to appreciate the different categories of thinking and in the second part to clarify the meaning of "miracle" in its proper biblical sense.

I THE NATURAL SCIENTIST AND THE BIBLICAL CONCEPT OF MIRACLE

1 The viewpoint of natural science

For the scientist all phenomena in our experience of the world take place according to established laws and

44

rules. Classical physics, with its causality confined to a closed system, that makes possible the assertion of the fixed "laws of nature," has been superseded and considerably modified in our century by the quantum theory and the theory of relativity. The so-called law of nature is valid in a strict sense only for a limited area of phenomena and for a definite quantitative order, since the atomic structure as well as astrophysics exhibit other relationships. Therefore, the laws of nature have been reduced more to "static rules"; but these attain in our world of experience such a high degree of certainty that for practical purposes they become equivalent to strict laws. It would be a mistake to apply to the area of miracle the infrastructure of matter used in this sphere.[1] This is likewise the case with parapsychology, which has attained a scientific rank and which also exhibits certain exceptional phenomena deviating from the sphere of ordinary experimental psychology. Here the theologian can hardly postulate a position for miracles that would be acknowledged by scientists themselves.

Another point becomes immediately clear. Natural science, on the whole, does not possess a method by

[1] For these questions see the work of H. van der Loos, *The Miracles of Jesus* (Leiden, 1965), which in the first part deals with the viewpoint of natural scientists and gives many further references. His own conclusion is valid: "The 'possibility' of miracles is just as problematic now as in the days of triumphal progress of classical physics. For all the present-day talk of a certain freedom in the events of the microcosm—which we call freedom because the movements are immeasurable and perhaps will remain so though that is still obscure—there is not a single reason for asserting that 'quantum physics has made miracles possible' or that 'a certain latitude' is left for miracles" (p. 63).

which it can come to an understanding of miracle. Natural science, understood as science, deals only with the sphere of the experimental, the measurable and the verifiable. When science considers actual phenomena, which are beyond observation, causality, and experimental verification, then it goes beyond its proper sphere. Its object is "nature based on experience"; its scientific method is fundamentally and essentially the summarizing of observations and data into rules and laws, and wherever possible, even though it is not necessary, formulating these laws mathematically. For these law-making processes it is important that the formulated laws which natural science deduces from its data be empirically reproducible, in order that they can be verified. Also, in cases where it is necessary, as in the transition from classical to quantum physics, they must be modifiable and expandable. Therefore, the experiment as a repeatable process and check plays a very meaningful role. Where unique and exceptional phenomena, which we designate as miracles, are dealt with, the scientist must work with his own hypotheses that classify these phenomena into categories of scientific causality. This is particularly true where causal relations are not able to be present. He cannot work with a miracle which is an exception to the rule of natural causality. Hence, he can discover in the asserted miracle no presupposition from which he could deduce a cause (which we call God) existing outside of the physically connecting causality. The supernatural cannot for him be an object of knowing. The words of a natural scientist might be quoted: "In summarizing, it may be said that natural science basically is not acquainted with and does not acknowledge a concept of miracle. It is an object of faith, and where the phenomenon appears it points to unusual spiritual powers which step beyond 'normal' and 'natural' actions."[2]

Certainly one can and must object to the scientist committing himself in this matter to the sphere of the "perceptible," which does not embrace the whole of reality. As one scholar notes,

It is understandable that a scientist, who makes an observation which appears to contradict the well-known laws of nature, will first search after unknown natural explanations. But as long as it is not possible for him to actually discover these, or at least make them probable, it is undoubtedly his right to designate the investigation as unexplainable. But it would be completely and absolutely unscientific to conclude that powers outside of nature are impossible (according to the principle that what may not be cannot be). That would exceed the justified area in which the natural scientist could make a statement.[3]

Consequently, according to the present concept of science, one cannot blame the scientist when he dismisses such a statement as belonging to the sphere of "faith."

At this point the problem of "knowledge and faith" arises, and it appears that both methods of science and

[2] This is a thesis taken from a lively discussion at a meeting of the "Paulus-Gesellschaft." It strives for an encounter between natural scientists and scholars of other intellectual areas. See "Wunder und Wissenschaft," Dokumente der Paulus-Gesellschaft, vol. 5 (München, 1963) 20, H. Schaefer, Heidelberg.

[3] A remark of R. Kautzky on the same occasion cited in note above, Dokumente (see p. 30).

faith stand irreconcilably opposed to each other. However, the believing scientist assures us that for one
who considers himself within the borders of his science,
the present-day scientific thinking is not an obstacle to
faith. As soon as one asks a question about man and
human existence, the scientific way of thinking does
not seem to be sufficient. Here we enter an area where
human-personal behavior compels us to look into other
ways of thinking. Philosophers and theologians are
called upon to explain the sense of human life and history. In many scientific fields such as psychology and
medicine, which are understood primarily as natural
sciences and work according to scientific methods,
questions arise from encountering man as a personal
being and from the treatment of man. For example, the
medical man remarks that in his science he investigates
physiological phenomena, but that beside a sick-bed
he collects many experiences that reach beyond scientific data. He does not call this "scientific knowledge," but rather "hermeneutic understanding."[4] Indeed, one can distinguish "explaining" nature from
"understanding" it. " 'Understanding' is all-embrac-
ing, it is teleologically directed, it seeks the last grounds
and values."[5] But the task of natural science is only
to investigate the phenomena and to explain them ac-

[4] R. Brühl (Trier) in the same discussion, *Dokumente* (see p.
159 f.); in a similar way other participants gave their opinion.
[5] H. van der Loos, *Miracles* 73; cf. also 78: "Even though the
scientist will never be able to 'explain' miracles, it will be possible for him to 'understand' miracles. This understanding is
an understanding of faith which does not regard nature as
something outside of God or as a part of God but as a creation
of God over which He, as Maker, is therefore also Lord. . . ."

cording to natural causality. Therefore, the discussion of miracles shocks the scientist and is unreasonable to him; he still needs to work without assuming miracles.

2 The standpoint of the Bible

The Bible when speaking of miracles takes a completely different position.[6] It is not acquainted with natural science in its modern sense, and thus reduces all events to the work of God. All that man observes and experiences in the world about him, as well as all that he experiences historically, is understood as the work of the creator and conservator of the world, who is also the Lord of human history. Hence, the biblical concept of miracle differs from the scientific one. Whatever astonishes and bewilders man can in the Bible connote a miracle, especially in the psalms where pious ones again and again extol their deliverance from personal misery and danger as the miracle of the good and merciful God. "I will praise you, O Lord,

[6] Literature: A. Richardson, *The Miracle Stories of the Gospels*, 3rd ed. (London, 1948); R. M. Grant, *Miracle and Natural Law in Graeco-Roman and Early Christian Thought* (Amsterdam, 1952); G. Delling, "Das Verständnis des Wunders im Neuen Testament," *Zeitschrift für systemat. Theol.* 24 (1955) 265-280; A. George, "Les miracles de Jésus dans les Évangiles synoptiques," *Lumière et Vie* 33 (1957) 7-24; T. A. Burkill, "The Notion of Miracle with Special Reference to St. Mark's Gospel," *ZNW* 50 (1959) 33-48; V. Hamp, "Genus litterarium in Wunderberichten," *Estudios Eccles.* 34 (1960) 361-366; J. Kallas, *The Significance of the Synoptic Miracles* (London, 1961); A. Vögtle, "Jesu Wunder einst und heute," *Bibel und Leben* 2 (1961) 234-254; H. van der Loos, *Miracles*; A. de Groot, *Das Wunder im Zeugnis der Bibel* (Salzburg, 1965).

with my whole heart; I will show forth all your marvelous works. . . . When my enemies are turned back, they shall fall and perish in your presence" (Ps 92:2ff.). "Many are your wonderful works which you have done and your thoughts towards us: Nothing can be compared to you, O Lord my God" (Ps 40:6). The prototype of all miracles is the deliverance of the people of Israel from slavery in Egypt. With a powerful arm God has worked "signs and wonders" which are reflected repeatedly in the writings of the Old Testament. Thus the events that we would dismiss in a purely "natural" way, as well as those that seem exceptional insofar as they interrupt the normal order of things and are contrary to the law of nature, are explained in the Bible as miracles. Therefore, the events that we would consider as miraculous phenomena—for example, curing the sick—need not in the Bible be treated as exceptional.

From this point of view we can better understand much of what is relative in the New Testament, as well as many of the works of Jesus. Certainly the men of that time were greatly impressed by these sudden and astonishing cures, which were not a part of ordinary, everyday life, and of course deemed them miracles. They believed that such cures, worked by the prayers of pious men, were possible. Many cures that Jesus performed were not beyond what one would expect from the prophets or great rabbis. God is able to work in many ways: through the natural powers of healing, through the extraordinary intercession of prayer, or even through the application of quasi-magical media. In pagan circles also "godly men" were credited with special powers through which they performed amazing cures of repugnant and horrifying illnesses, often attributed to the influences of demons. In Jewish circles, therefore, Jesus, by curing infirmities and casting out devils, could be identified as a man distinguished before God, one considered close to God, a religious man gifted with powerful intercession—whereas in pagan circles he would be a man filled with magical powers. Thus, it is difficult for us today to determine the extent to which these actions were cures that can be explained naturally or whether they were events that are unexplainable by natural science.

Since the entire past was biased in presenting the cures and miracle stories of the New Testament, they were told in a stereotype form. In the Old Testament there are special literary forms for such stories, for example, the miracle of the Exodus from Egypt and those performed by the prophets or men of God. In the New Testament the healing of the sick and the casting out of devils are presented in a consistent type of narrative. The so-called form-criticism method has investigated the characteristic features of such passages and sees in them signs of the many traditions about Jesus that might have been orally narrated and then set down in written form. But here the question arises whether they were handed down with historical faithfulness, only formulated by the first believers, or actually constructed by the primitive Christian community in order to emphasize the effect of Jesus' historical appearance. Nevertheless, from an investigation of the numerous traditions, it can hardly be disputed that Jesus did perform sensational cures, and today even the most critical investigators admit this.

The distinguishing characteristics of Jesus' work can be

established through this form-criticism method of examination and the comparison of the history of religions. Jesus did not use any magical manipulations;[6a] he did not exert force in regard to the sick; nor did he utter many words. But rather he healed the sick and cast out evil spirits with a word of command. To his Jewish contemporaries this was something special and very exciting. "What is this? A new teaching! With authority he commands even the unclean spirits, and they obey him" (Mk 1:27). They seem to acknowledge distinguishing characteristics in Jesus, for it seems clear that an exceptional power had been given to him. A comparison between ancient narratives of Jewish and other wonder-workers and the gospels reveals striking differences. For example, there is a story told of the god Asklepios, who had his sanctuary in Epidauros. He let a mother give birth to a child after she had been pregnant five years. As soon as the child was born it was able to jump about as a four-year-old.[7] No such spectacular miracles are reported of Jesus. Another story is from the life of the wonder-worker Apollonius of Tyana. It is told that during a feast a possessed boy broke out in loud, indecent laughter. Apollonius said, "You do not commit this outrage, but the devil, who rules you without your knowledge."

[6a] The means used in some cures that seem magical to us (Mk 7:32-37 or Jn 9:6-7) were viewed as practices of a doctor at that time. Jesus accommodated himself to popular views to assure people of his healing. By the context it is clear that the healing is not the effect of a natural process but the work of God.

[7] Inscriptiones Graecae Nr. 951, quoted by P. Fiebig, *Antike Wundergeschichten*, Kleine Texte 79 (Bonn, 1921) 3.

Apollonius looked fiercely and sharply into the boy's eyes. The devil began to wail and curse to free himself from the boy. But Apollonius dramatically turned his full anger upon the spirit and commanded him to depart with a visible sign. The devil replied, "I will topple the monument." And that is exactly what happened.[8] Yet another incident comes from Flavius Josephus, who relates how Eleazar held a ring under the nose of a sick man—a ring that contained roots given to him by Solomon. He let the sick person smell the ring and then proceeded to draw out the evil spirit from his nose. The possessed man collapsed; and Eleazar, cursing the spirit in the name of Solomon, told him never again to enter the man.[9] Compared to these dramatic, magical exorcisms, the New Testament narratives are much more realistic. Jesus did not use a magical medium or formula but rather commanded the evil spirit—and it simply obeyed him. However, there are a few events that appear to be colored or elaborated by popular representation. The woman with the hemorrhage is confident that she need only touch the hem of Jesus' garment to be cured (Mk 5:25-34); or Jesus commands a legion of devils to enter a herd of pigs (Mk 5:11–14).[9a] In these cases the circumstances and environment of the people are reflected in the narratives.

[8] Philostratus, *Vita Apollonii*, vol. 4, 20; ed. Loeb, F. C. Conybeare, vol. 1, 388 ff.).

[9] Flavius Josephus, *Ant.* VIII, 46f.; ed. B. Niese, vol. 2, 186 f.

[9a] In regard to this story see C. H. Cave, "The Obedience of Unclean Spirits," *New Testament Studies* 11 (1964, 1965) 93-97. The author thinks that there is an allusion in Mark 5:11-14 to Exodus 14:27 ff. In this case the scene had an allegorical sense.

For this reason it is difficult to distinguish the historical works of Jesus from the old representations. If one compares the biblical narratives with today's view, it is understandable that the historical critic has his doubts as to exactly "how it was." Likewise the scientist will see no reason to abandon the presumption that all could be explained without miracles.

It must be emphasized that for the first Christians the miracles of Jesus as such were not the basis for their belief in him as the Messiah and Son of God. They first came to believe through the resurrection of Jesus. This event, confirmed by many reliable witnesses, was for them the foundation of their faith in the crucified. In the light of Jesus' resurrection, the cures and miracles of his earthly life were put into a new perspective. Looking back, they acknowledged in these events Jesus' hidden divine power and authority. But how far can we rely on these witnesses of the risen Lord? Here, too, they could have reported their experiences merely in the contemporary manner of thinking and speaking. Furthermore, an event such as that would be difficult to describe. Therefore, the narratives telling of the risen Lord vary: some are reserved, some exaggerated, and some realistic. Certainly one can and must acknowledge the improbability that the narratives of the resurrection witnesses are traced only to subjective visions. Above all, it remains incomprehensible that the utterly confused disciples could, after the terrible end of Jesus' life, awaken their faith in the risen Lord. But critical scholars will not be able to produce final historical certainty, because the event itself transcends ordinary empirical experiences and empirical categories themselves. For scientists this fundamental miracle of the Christian faith stands outside of their scientific investigation. It is not an object of scientific knowledge, but rather an object of faith.

From the standpoint of biblical research we are also compelled to conclude that the miracles of the New Testament are not the object of scientific investigation, not at least natural scientific knowledge. At the most, they are to a certain degree the object of historical research. Therefore, it appears aimless to discuss the miracles in the New Testament on a scientific basis. There are many veils separating us from a clear view of the singular events of the past. One such veil is historical distance, which makes it impossible for us to let the series of events once again pass before our eyes; then there is the literary style of the narratives that transmit the events in a manner understandable to and characteristic of the ancient peoples; and finally we have the other trend of thought which is rooted in our changing notion of the world. Only if we are prepared to take up the fundamental view of the Bible, can we come to a starting point for biblical statements. First, God directs all events in nature and history. Second, the observation and experiences in the sense of the natural sciences may not exclusively and completely determine our knowledge. Third, our human existence demands a more comprehensive view of the world, embracing all that happens in it and especially human existence itself. Therefore, we will ask in the second part, which is particularly important for us as believers, what is the meaning of miracles in the view of the Bible itself.

II THE MEANING OF MIRACLE IN THE NEW TESTAMENT

As in the Old Testament, miracles in the New are treated within the context of the salvific action of God as it is grasped in faith. But the New Testament miracles preserve a certain dignity and relevance, since they come through God's latest ambassador, the eschatological prophet and bearer of our salvation, Jesus Christ. Therefore, they become signs and witnesses of God for the eschatological perfection and the salvation foretold by the prophets.[10] Since they give witness to the authority of Jesus who bestows salvation, they gain a special Christological significance. They have a special declarative power for the hidden nature and person of Jesus. In this function they should instill faith, as well as reveal the dignity and glory of Christ to those who do believe. To the nonbeliever, on the contrary, they hide the meaning of the event perfected in Christ. These are the points of view we wish to consider more closely.

1 Miracles as eschatological signs of salvation history

In the tradition of the evangelists, there is clear proof that Jesus himself considered his cures and exorcisms, miraculous works, and acts of authority as signs that the time of salvation had come to pass. When John the Baptist is in prison and sends his disciples to ask "Are

[10] See the books of A. Richardson, J. Kallas, H. van der Loos et al., mentioned above.

you he who should come, or shall we look for another?"
Jesus answers, "Go and report to John what you see
and hear: the blind receive their sight and the lame
walk, lepers are cleansed and the deaf hear, and the
dead are raised up, and the poor have good news
preached to them. And blessed is he who takes no offense at me" (Mt 11:1-6). Here Jesus does not use his
own words, but rather refers to the expressions of the
prophet Isaias (35:5f., 61:1). What the great prophet
of salvation foretold as the time salvation would come
is fulfilled now in the works of Jesus. God himself proclaims that the time is fulfilled, his kingdom is at hand.
If people see these events with eyes of faith, they can
find the meaning of God's message. Here we are no
longer dealing with the acts of certain prophets or with
the cures of some great men of God. But we can and
should recognize God's action at the beginning of the
time of our salvation, at the dawn of the kingdom of
God. The works of Jesus do not necessarily lead men to
faith. These exceptional events call each man to his
own personal decision. Thus Jesus warns, "Blessed is
he who takes no offense at me." The same holds true
when Jesus casts out devils: "If it is by the finger of
God that I cast out demons, then the kingdom of God
has come upon you" (Lk 11:20). The meaning of his
work is clear. He announces the approaching reign of
God, which is opposed by the powers of evil. According to Jewish thinking these powers are assembled
under the reign of Satan and reveal themselves in the
phenomena of diabolical possession.

The outstanding miracles—which we would denote as
"natural miracles"—have another meaning in the

Bible. The multiplication of loaves is not meant simply to reveal Jesus' power to satisfy the hunger of many men with a little bread. We should not interpret it merely as an exception to the law of nature (the conservation of energy) brought about through the immediate intercession of God in a natural event. It has a much deeper and more significant background which is explained from salvation history. In the Old Testament God did not let the people of Israel starve in the desert, but gave them heavenly bread ("manna"). In the New Testament God's Promised One gathers the People of God in the desert and prepares them for the Lord's banquet. This becomes evident in Mark 6, where Jesus refers to the situation of Israel in the desert. The other events whereby Jesus appears to manifest his divinity—the transfiguration, the walking on the water, the calming of the storm—must be seen in like manner. They do not merely demonstrate the superiority of Jesus over the forces of nature, but also reveal the divine nature of Jesus that shines forth from the glorified Lord as he appears to his disciples. The narratives expose that the closest disciples did not immediately comprehend each mystery-filled event in the earthly life of Jesus, but—as the believing reader—they also understood such divine manifestations of Jesus only in the light of the resurrection.

What has been said will become more clear to us if we observe that Jesus always chooses not to perform so-called exhibition miracles. In all the gospels the facts testify that Jesus refused to accommodate the unbelieving Jews with a "sign from heaven." Although Jesus works exceptional miracles visible to all, men who do not recognize in his deed the hand of God will not be-

lieve. Jesus says, "An evil and adulterous [that is, god-
less] generation seeks for a sign; but no sign shall be
given to it except the sign of the prophet Jonah"
(Mt 12:39). This "sign of Jonah" certainly means his
future coming in glory, which will open the eyes of
mankind. But when this comes to pass, the sign will
no longer lead them to a personal decision of faith but
will pass judgment on them because they did not believe the earthly Jesus.[11] In a word, Jesus always refuses to perform a miracle that would urge men to believe in him; therefore, the wondrous events of his
earthly life could not have had this meaning. They
are and remain signs of God, which reveal his purpose
of offering salvation to man, but they are also signs
pointing to a future fulfillment of the world. Jesus
thus heals the sick and casts out many devils, but he
does not give health to *all* who are sick or completely
abolish the suffering in the world.

2 The miracles of Jesus as Christological signs

Perhaps Jesus actually intended his miracles to be
understood as signs of God indicative of the approaching time of salvation. But his message cannot be separated from his person. These are simply miracles which
he worked and which raise the question "Who is he
that he has the power to perform these things?" His
community of believers—only after his resurrection—
understood clearly that the miracles do not merely represent God's merciful action toward man, but they also

[11] Cf. J. Jeremias, "'Ιωνᾶς," *ThWNT*, 3 (1939) 411-413; T. Mer-
ton, *The Sign of Jonas* (New York, 1953); A. Vögtle, "Der
Spruch vom Jonaszeichen," *Synoptische Studien*, Festschrift für
A. Wikenhauser (Freiburg, 1954) 230-277.

give witness to Jesus as the awaited bearer of salvation and only Son of God. This is also reflected in the writings of the evangelists. Throughout the synoptic gospels the evangelists in their own way portray the person of Jesus by his miracles; consequently, in Luke, who writes for the Gentile Christians and Greek readers, they appear as merciful acts of a divine doctor. In a summarizing passage in the Acts of the Apostles he writes, "He went about doing good and healing all that were oppressed of the devil, for God was with him" (Acts 10:38). Matthew sees the miracles of Jesus more from the standpoint of salvation history, in which the God of the Old Testament worked miracles to help and rescue his people. Hence, he arranges ten miracles within chapters 8 and 9. The number *ten* calls to mind the ten miraculous plagues that God worked in Egypt before the Exodus; in the New Testament these would be ten acts of salvation performed by the Messiah at the beginning of a new and final age of salvation. In Mark, then, we find that he desires to emphasize the hidden glory of Jesus, the Son of God.

The evangelist John has drawn the final conclusions that the miracles of Jesus reveal the glory of the only begotten Son. For him miracles are Christological signs directly declaring something about the person of Jesus. He consciously uses the expression "signs," since the external events manifest something deeper: Jesus revealing himself in his capacity as the prophet and bearer of salvation, the divine Logos become flesh.[12]

[12] See R. Schnackenburg, *Das Johannesevangelium*, vol. 1 (Freiburg, 1965), exc. 4, 344-356, with further bibliographic references.

Thus the healing of the man born blind reveals him as "the Light of the World" (Jn 9:5) and the raising of Lazarus from the dead reveals him as "the Resurrection and the Life" (11:25). John adds to the miracle of the multiplication of loaves—also preserved in the tradition of the other evangelists—a long revelation in which Jesus bears witness to himself as the "Bread from Heaven," the "living and life giving Bread" (6:32-58). He reproaches the Jews because they wanted only to eat the loaves and be filled. Whoever truly understood the sign indeed acknowledged Jesus to be "the Bread from Heaven," which is by far greater than the manna in the desert (6:32f.). Here then is the deeper meaning of the miracle, as the believing community would realize after Easter when they reflected on the works of the earthly Jesus.

However, since these earthly "signs" of Jesus dealt with his real acts, they became "witnesses" establishing his claims. The Evangelist himself confesses he has written down these signs so that readers might believe Jesus to be the Christ, the Son of God, and believing they might have life in his name (Jn 20:31). We see more clearly what argumentative force these signs and witnesses possess. Jesus "had done so many signs before them, yet they did not believe in him" (12:37). These extraordinary miracles, which the believers did not question, could not convince skeptical men of Jesus' mission and his divine nature. He repeatedly reproached them, "If I am not doing the works of my Father, then do not believe me; but if I do them, even though you do not believe me, believe the works that you may know and understand that the Father is in me

and I in the Father" (10:37f.). To his disciples at the
Last Supper Jesus says, "If I had not come and spoken
to them they would not have sin. . . . If I had not done
among them the works which no one else did, they
would not have sin; but now they have seen and hated
both me and my Father" (15:22ff.). Therefore, the
works or signs become an indictment against the unbelievers and a profound revelation for the believers.
Now we come to the last point of view which we must
consider.

3 The miracles of Jesus as crucial signs separating believers from nonbelievers

There is an eschatological action of God that takes
place in the miraculous works of Jesus. Through their
exceptional quality and lucidity they call on men to
acknowledge this action. But they do not exercise con-
straining influence compelling the answer of faith.
Jesus' words pose an unavoidable question by urgently
appealing to our faith in his message of salvation. His
words do not, however, dispense men from the decision of faith. We could say that the preaching of Jesus,
confirmed by God through cures and miracles, motivates and enlightens men to believe in Jesus. But, as a
historical event permitting reflection and personal decision, it remains obscure so that unbelievers will constantly find a foundation to oppose the revelation of
God. This is how the primitive Church sees it. Another
question perhaps is this: Influenced by epistemological
difficulties, the present state of knowledge, and his per-

sonal problems, to what extent is contemporary man capable or incapable of faith?

For the modern man—particularly the scientist, who opposes the New Testament accounts of Jesus' miracles as well as the decisive witness of Jesus' disciples to the resurrection as the greatest miracle—there are many more obstacles barring understanding than for the man in the past. Modern man not only has to "believe without seeing," as the readers of the gospels in the second and third generation of Christianity had to do, but also needs to make allowances for the ancient notion of miracles. With his new scientific notion of the world he opposes a simpler and less complex mode of thinking that accepts miracles at their face value. Nevertheless, he basically does not find himself in a different situation from that of the early Christians, because the acceptance of a crucified and resurrected Jesus was also a challenge to their human way of thinking, "a stumbling block to Jews and folly to Gentiles" (1 Cor 1:23). Today as in the past, faith depends upon the position we assume in regard to the crucified and resurrected Lord. And we ask today, as did the men in the past, whether our faith is a "hoping against hope," a belief in God who "gives life to the dead and calls into existence the things that do not exist" (Rom 4:17).

CHAPTER IV

Freedom in the Thought of the Apostle Paul

The problem of freedom leads man, who wishes to understand the existing world and his own personal existence, to urgent and inevitable questions.[1] Knowledge that the strict determinism in natural science is no longer valid today, as in the past, is valuable but it has no immediate significance for man. Certainly to con-

[1] For various points of view see E. Welty, *Gemeinschaft und Einzelmensch* (Salzburg, 1935); *Freedom, Its Meaning by Croce, Mann, Whitehead, and others*, ed. R. N. Anshem (New York, 1940); H. de Lubac, *Esprit et liberté: Surnaturel* (Paris, 1946); R. Egenter, *Von der Freiheit der Kinder Gottes* (Freiburg, 1949); J. Michl, *Freiheit und Bindung* (München, 1950); R. Bultmann, "Die Bedeutung des Gedankens der Freiheit für die abendländische Kultur," *Glauben und Verstehen*, vol. 2 (Tübingen, 1952) 274-293; M. Pohlenz, *Griechische Freiheit* (Heidelberg, 1955); G. Siewerth, *Die Freiheit und das Gute* (Freiburg, 1959); B. Welte, *Uber das Böse* (Freiburg, 1959); K. Rahner, *Schriften zur Theologie*, vol. 2 (Einsiedeln, 1959) 95-114, 247-277; C. Spicq, *Charité et liberté dans le Nouveau Testament* (Paris, 1961); "La liberté religieuse," *Lumière et Vie* 69 (1964).

sider man as a machine was a misconception, and likewise, today, to construe a machine as though it were a man and to define this robot as a higher thing is a perversion. Such misconceptions reveal that man has another nature and must realize his proper human existence in another way.

In the question of freedom only human freedom is at stake. There is a double aspect to freedom, external or social and internal or individual, both giving rise to new problems. There is a lack of external freedom which we in the "free West" wish to overcome. Many men believe in the Declaration of Independence, guaranteeing the rights of "life, liberty and the pursuit of happiness," as well as in the Bill of Rights guaranteeing freedom of speech, freedom of religion, and freedom of press. These are fundamental human rights that the Christian faith defends but that are not primarily the subject of the religious thought found in the Bible. Beyond these there arises an inner freedom or lack of freedom within man himself. Why, for example, guarantee external freedom of movement and protection from arbitrary arrest, if a man motivated by evil in his heart commits crimes for which the state must sentence him to prison? Why acknowledge the right to life and bodily integrity if man is subject to suffering and always sees death before him? Religion is concerned more with these inner aspects of freedom. Religion considers the forces of suffering and death to which man is exposed, as well as his inclinations and passions that limit inner freedom and plunge him into sin and guilt. Therefore, when we speak of moral and religious freedom we mean this inner freedom, not the external or social aspects of freedom. It is in this sense that the Apostle Paul speaks of freedom.

Man often feels himself helplessly confronted by the powers that threaten his existence. Paul deeply experienced and suffered the alienated existence of a man in "this world." It is a world where the powers of destruction determine the existence of man. At the end of a moving description of man's inner confusion he cries out, "Wretched man that I am! Who will deliver me from this body of death?" But he joyfully continues, "Thanks be to God through Jesus Christ our Lord!" (Rom 7:24f.). The answer that Paul had found for himself is clear and definite; it is the answer of Christian faith. But in order to clarify his thoughts about this aspect of freedom we start from the words written to the Galatians, "For freedom Christ has set us free; stand fast therefore, and do not submit again to a yoke of slavery" (Gal 5:1). Here we have three ideas. First, Christ has set us free and has delivered us from the yoke of slavery. Second, we stand now in freedom and we should remain in freedom. Third, he has set us free for freedom and calls us to further freedom. The last statement may not appear intelligible, but in order to understand it we must first consider the two previous statements.

I FREEDOM FROM THE "YOKE OF SLAVERY"

What does Paul mean by freedom from slavery? This much is clear: it is not an external lack of freedom, for example, political oppression, social slavery, captivity, or similar things. It is much more involved with the inner situation of man. To understand this we must realize the occasion and purpose of his epistle to the Galatians. One could call it a document of Christian freedom.[2]

Before becoming Christians the Galatians were pagans who openly engaged in a kind of astrological cult. They worshiped the so-called world elements (Gal 4:9, cf.3) which they perhaps imagined to be types of cosmic powers directing the universe according to laws and demanding man to adapt himself to the cosmic order. This appears to us today as paganism based on a mythological notion of the world. Does Paul simply want to say that Christ has freed us from such void ideas and hallucinations? No, the Apostle is not referring to the Galatians' erroneous conceptions about the stars and their influence upon men. He speaks of these things only because the Galatians through this cult were in-

[2] For the notion of freedom in the New Testament, and particularly by Paul, see W. Brandt, *Freiheit im Neuen Testament* (München, 1932); H. Schlier, "ἐλεύθερος" *ThWNT* 2 (1935) 484-500; E. Gulin, "Die Freiheit in der Verkündigung des Paulus," *Zeitschrift für systematische Theologie* 18 (1941) 458-481; C. H. Dodd, *Gospel and Law*, Bampton Lectures, Columbia University (New York, 1951) and "Ἔννομος Χριστοῦ," *Studia Paulina in honorem J. de Zwaan* (Haarlem, 1953) 96-110; G. Bornkamm, "Die christliche Freiheit," *Das Ende des Gesetzes* (München, 1952) 133-138; R. Bultmann, *Theologie des Neuen Testaments* 3rd ed. (Tübingen, 1958) 331-353; S. Lyonnet, *Liberté chrétienne et loi de l'esprit selon S. Paul* (Rome, 1954) and English translation, *St. Paul: Liberty and Law* (Rome, 1962); Ch. de Beus, *Paulus, Apostel der Vrijheid* (Amsterdam, *circa.* 1953); H. Schlier, "Über das vollkommene Gesetz der Freiheit," *Die Zeit der Kirche* (Freiburg, 1956) 193-206; J. Cambier, "La liberté chrétienne selon S. Paul," *Studia Evangelica* 2 (Berlin, 1964) 315-353; R. N. Longenecker, *Paul, Apostle of Liberty* (New York, 1964).

ternally bound and enslaved. He tells them they are free from these things and have become free sons of God through God's Son Jesus Christ (4:17-7). One actually grasps Paul's thoughts when he warns and adjures the Galatians in the situation wherein they find themselves. He does not warn them about reverting to paganism but about falling prey to a false doctrine. Fake Jewish-Christian teachers had entered the Galatian community and had persuaded the newly converted Christians to let themselves be circumcised and to assume the burden of the Jewish law.

This is very significant. For Paul, a former Jew, circumcision and law now signify the same as the pagan cult! One sees clearly that not only the mythological world-power but also every constraint condemning man to inner impotency deprives him of his internal freedom. After his conversion from Judaism to the Christian faith, Paul sees the Mosaic law of Sinai as such an ominous constraint that excludes man from salvation (3:23f.). The Jewish law (the Nomos) is for him an element limited to a certain time (3:19)—one that actually had a role in God's plan of salvation, but was not intended to lead man to salvation.[3] Therefore, Paul says, "If (on Sinai) a law had been given that could give life, then righteousness would indeed be by the

[3] C. P. Bläser, *Das Gesetz bei Paulus* (Münster, 1941); G. Bornkamm, *Ende des Gesetzes* 51-69; R. Bultmann, *Theologie* 260-270; W. Gutbrod, *"νόμος," ThWN* 4 (1942) 1061-1070; E. Jüngel, "Das Gesetz zwischen Adam und Christus," *Zeitschrift für Theologie und Kirche* 60 (1963) 42-74; I. Beck, "Altes und neues Gesetz," *Münchener Theol. Zeitschrift* 15 (1964) 127-142; A. J. Bandstra, *The Law and the Elements of the World* (Kampen, Netherlands, 1964).

law. But the scripture consigned all things to sin" (3:21f.). In other words, the law could command man, but it could not give the power to execute these commands. Therefore, it doomed him to sin. This was the very sin against which the law warned him and threatened him with eternal punishment. Thus Paul speaks of the "curse of the law": "For it is written, 'Cursed be every one who does not abide by all things written in the book of the law, and do them' " (3:10). He who frees himself through Christ from the curse of the law and then again freely places himself under the Jewish law by undergoing circumcision, actually lets himself be constrained under the yoke of slavery. It must be emphasized that this severe criticism of the Jewish law originates from a world-view which is dominated by salvation history. For Paul, then, it becomes possible and effective only after his conversion to the Christian faith.

This brief treatment of the epistle to the Galatians is sufficient to understand what Paul considers the actual slavery of man. It is an existence powerlessly and helplessly alienated among the powers of evil. In the epistle to the Romans he refers to these powers of destruction as sin and death: "Through one man sin came into the world and through sin death" (5:12). Here he explicitly has in mind Adam, but he considers sin and death the fatal powers that since the time of Adam threaten and destroy our very human existence. Man today is unwilling to recognize these powers that darken his existence. He considers death as a power of destruction annihilating his existence, and he seeks to overcome the fear of death. But Paul understands the power of death more comprehensively and deeply; for him physical death is only a prototype of what the actual death of man is, namely, the failure to attain the goal of his life, the exclusion from God's eternal life. The power of death triumphs completely over man if with the death of the body no further hope exists and all is truly lost. But if man in spite of physical death can gain the life of God, then death loses its sting. Before Christ came, sin placed man under the judgment of God and robbed him of hope. Man who is defenselessly and hopelessly alienated by sin stands in a frightful situation—condemned to death. "Now the sting of death is sin and the power of sin is the law," says the Apostle in another passage (1 Cor 15:56), that is, sin draws man into the full power of death, but sin itself becomes effective through the law which demands us to fulfil God's will but gives no power to accomplish the demands of the law.

Only a man of faith reaches this point of view. The secularized man sees only natural death and denies sin with its consequence for the final determination of man. In this way a purely natural philosophy of existence cannot truly free man from the fear of existence. If it is only physical death that stands as an inevitable fact before every man, then there is no hope. But Christian faith brings hope to this desperate situation. It is quite understandable that Christian faith cannot console those who reject the true Christian concept of existence. For it is a deeper meaning of human existence: death in its proper sense is not a physical annihilation; it is the death of man's true life, that true spiritual life binding him to God, who is eternal life.

The actual fear man has is not the dread of the end, but the fear of God's judgment that condemns his conduct and damns him. Paul treats this metaphysical situation of man, exposing the final and most hidden lack of freedom.

II OUR FREEDOM IN CHRIST

Christ has freed us from this helpless slavery, and he who belongs to Christ experiences this freedom. Paul describes Christ's act of liberation very plainly. The law threatening death had no claim on Christ because he had not transgressed it. He removed the curse of the law, taking upon himself the shameful death of the cross. "Christ redeemed us from the curse of the law, having become a curse for us; for it is written, 'Cursed be everyone who hangs on a tree' " (Gal 3:13). Since the law can no longer enforce upon us the punishment of eternal death, we are removed from the fate of death. Through Christ we have gained the real possibility of escaping the condemning judgment of God. We may again hope to participate in eternal life. God, in Christ, has reconciled the world to himself by not reckoning our sins against us (2 Cor 5:19). It pleased him to reconcile the universe to himself through Christ in whom he made peace through the blood of his cross (Col 1:20). In such way Paul describes the unique redemptive act of Christ under the same aspect, but in different images.[4]

[4] Cf. R. G. Bandas, *The Master-Idea of St. Paul or the Redemption* (Bruges, 1925); G. Wiencke, *Paulus über Jesu Tod* (Gütersloh, 1939); K. H. Schelkle, *Die Passion Jesu in der Verkündigung des Neuen Testaments* (Heidelberg, 1949); A. Kirchgäss-

It is difficult to comprehend that "one dies for all" (2 Cor 5:14). This act of substitution is and remains a mystery of faith. It is credible only if we consider Jesus Christ as the Second Adam, the head of a new mankind (Rom 5:12-21; 1 Cor 15:22, 45-49). Even then the cross remains a stumbling block (Gal 5:11;1 Cor 1:23). But if we take the profound thought of revelation seriously, then we should not be surprised that God acted in this way. The thoughts of God revealed to us through the Bible are different from those of man. His ways and decisions are unfathomable to human investigation. Paul recognizes in this the hidden wisdom of God (1 Cor 2:7f.). It is the paradox of the religion of the cross that God wished to save us through the foolishness of the cross, inasmuch as the world had not recognized his wisdom in creation. "Since, in the wisdom of God, the world did not know God through wisdom, it pleased God by the folly of what we preach to save those who believe" (1 Cor 1:21). How do we attain the freedom that Christ has gained for us? How is this freedom concretely realized? Paul answers these questions. In baptism, he says, the spirit of God is poured out upon us and the divine spirit of life fills us, directing and stimulating us to lead a life

ner, *Erlösung und Sünde im Neuen Testament* (Freiburg, 1950) 100-121; Ph. Seidensticker, *Lebendiges Opfer (Röm 12, 1)* (Münster, 1954); D. M. Stanley, *Christ's Resurrection in Pauline Soteriology* (Rome, 1961); K. Romaniuk, *L'amour du Père et du Fils dans la sotériologie de Saint Paul* (Rome, 1961); S. Lyonnet, *De Vocabulario Redemptionis* (Rome, 1960); J. Dupont, *La réconciliation dans la théologie de S. Paul* (Louvain, 1953; L. Sabourin, *Rédemption sacrificielle* (Bruges, 1961); D. E. H. Whiteley, *The Theology of St. Paul* (Oxford, 1964) 130-154.

according to the will of God and promising us eternal life with God. This is easily said but not too easily comprehended. In the Bible the spirit of God is a reality, a dynamic force working in the world and in man. The world has been created through his creative spirit, which bears and preserves the universe. "You send forth your spirit, they are created, and you renew the face of the earth" (Ps 104:30). According to Paul, a new creation of man takes place in baptism: "If any one is in Christ, he is a new creature; the old man has passed away; behold, the new has come" (2 Cor 5:17). The "old man" who was a slave to the forces of sin and death is in baptism crucified with Christ. If we die with Christ, we shall also live with him (Rom 6:6, 8). Through an act of God the state of the unredeemed man leading to eternal death is abolished and transformed into a new possibility and hope for life. Thus, the helpless enslavement to the powers of destruction has been overcome and a new understanding of existence, with the hope of salvation, has been given to us. It is, of course, not a question of a physical transformation, for the abilities and powers of the natural man continue to exist. Rather, a divine power has been given to him, which can banish all evil and darkness. The law, insofar as it contains the salvation-bearing directives of God, also continues to exist, but now it no longer encounters a man who stands powerlessly and helplessly before its demands. It confronts a *new* man who is being renewed "according to the image of his creator" (Col 3:10). The spirit of God is a power in man motivating him to good. Here Paul speaks of a new "law" which is effective in us: "The law of the Spirit

of life in Christ Jesus has set me free from the law of
sin and death" (Rom 8:2). Note the different meaning
of "law" in the beginning and end of this terse
statement.[5] The "law of sin and death" was the ancient
law, an external and impassable code of proscriptions,
a burdening yoke from which we are now freed. But the
"law" of life in Christ is not an external force, but an
inner impulse to good coming from the Holy Spirit.
Led and empowered by the spirit of God, we can put
to death the sinful works of the flesh (Rom 8:13) and
become sons of God—"For you did not receive the
spirit of slavery to fall back into fear, but you have
received the spirit of sonship. When we cry: 'Abba,
Father!' it is the Spirit himself bearing witness to our
spirit that we are children of God" (Rom 8:15f.). In
order to understand this, we must free ourselves from
whatever spiritualistic concept of spirit Greek thought
might suggest to us. It is not a question of a new conviction but that of a new power which God, the ever
working and living spirit, bestows upon us. As modern
men, we are skeptical. Is there truly such a spirit of
God? Does a new creation of man actually take place
in baptism? Do we perceive something of the power of
the Holy Spirit that is bestowed upon us? To unbelieving men we can prove nothing, and even as believing
men we will not always *perceive* the spirit of God. But
if we do lead a life of faith and recall to ourselves in
prayer the gift given to us by God, we can and will have

[5] Besides the commentaries, cf. especially S. Lyonnet, *Liberté
chrétienne* and his "Rom 8, 2-4 à la lumière de Jérémie 31 et d'
Ezéchiel 35-39," *Mélanges E. Tisserant vol. 1* (Rome, 1964) 311-
323.

the same experience as Paul: the Holy Spirit himself bears witness to our spirit, that we are children of God (Rom 8:16). The efficacy of the new existence given to us by God depends upon our not opposing the divine spirit in us, but rather upon allowing ourselves to be guided by him. Then the Holy Spirit himself produces his "fruits": "Love, joy, peace, patience, kindness, goodness, faithfulness, gentleness, self-control" (Gal 5:22f.). Or, as Paul puts it, "If we live by the Spirit, let us also walk by the Spirit" (Gal 5:25). The new understanding of Christian existence is paradoxical: in his naked naturalness and creatureliness the Christian understands himself to be radically deprived of freedom; but created anew in Christ, through the spirit of God, he knows himself to be transformed by a new freedom.

III MORAL AND ESCHATOLOGICAL FREEDOM

The effects of the Christian state of freedom are the last elements that we shall treat. Genuine freedom is not only liberation *from* something but also a lasting freedom *for* something. Paul uses "Set free for freedom." What does he mean? He sees freedom not only as an acquired good but also as a task and aim. Using freedom is much more difficult than possessing it. To use freedom in the right way means to use it for good. This is the moral freedom we have already mentioned. On the level of Christian faith it appears otherwise: it is not a question of whether man by his natural powers and abilities can realize the good. For a Christian it becomes a fact that this effort with the power of God's spirit is not hopeless. Paul must have repeatedly fought against misunderstandings in regard to his doctrine of freedom. Libertines had their own interpretations: "All things are lawful for me" (1 Cor 6:12); "Let us sin because we are not under law but under grace!" (Rom 6:15); or even, "Let us continue in sin that grace may abound" (Rom 6:1). Paul determinedly prevents such dangerous slogans. Christian freedom, he says, is not a license for licentiousness. "You were called to freedom, brethren; only do not use your freedom as an opportunity for the flesh!" (Gal 5:13). Freedom gives man the true dignity of his person and identifies him as a son of God. Concretely, Paul sees this freedom for good realized in love: "Bear one another's burdens and so fulfil the law of Christ!" (Gal 6:2). Here again we hear of a "law," the law of Christ. We must interpret it the same as the "law of the Spirit of life in Christ Jesus" (Rom 8:2). This does not mean a pressing constrain but a fostering love (2 Cor 5:14f.), given to us by the Holy Spirit (Rom 5:5). This love urges and motivates us to love our neighbor, "For the whole law is fulfilled in one word, 'You shall love your neighbor as yourself'" (Gal 5:14). Thus, the very meaning of the old law is now fulfilled in a new way through the power of the Holy Spirit. The law of love places the Christian under an obligation, but only to make him free. We can fulfill it if we do not resist the prompting action of God's spirit.

Now we look once again at eschatological freedom. Christian freedom on earth is still imperfect. The final freedom is given to the Christian in the end when every power impeding salvation, even the "last enemy," the

power of death, is finally annihilated (1 Cor 15:26).
Then the full glory of God's Son comes forth. The rest
of creation will also participate in this "eschatological
freedom." In Romans 8:21 the Apostle says, "The creation itself will be set free from its bondage to decay and
obtain the glorious liberty of the children of God."
How this liberty of the whole creation is to be understood is not disclosed, but a hint lies in the word
"glory" which points to the transfiguration.[6] All im-
perfection and corruption is taken away from human
existence in the world to come. But for redeemed mankind it is not merely a perfection of one's natural state
but also of one's moral disposition. There is a connection between the present state of our redemption
and that of the future. The present state of freedom
also gives a Christian the possibility to gain perfect
freedom in the future, which will lead to glory. Theologically, we can simply say that the *posse non peccare*
will then become a *non posse peccare*. Liberated from
sin and death, the Christian stands in a preliminary,
but real, freedom whose power he can already experience as moral freedom, but whose glory will be revealed and realized only when the final fulfillment
takes place.

It might appear that such an understanding of existence is far removed from the reality of the world. To
do away with this doubt, we shall compare the Pauline

[6] Cf. H. M. Biedermann, *Die Erlösung der Schöpfung beim
Apostel Paulus* (Würzburg, 1940); R. Potter, "The Expectation
of the Creature," *Scripture* 4 (1951) 256-262; H. K. Gieraths,
"Knechtschaft und Freiheit der Schöpfung" (dissertation, Bonn,
1956); W. D. Stacey, "Paul's Certainties, II: God's Purpose in
Creation," *Expository Times* 69 (1958) 178-181.

concept of freedom with that which prevailed in Paul's environment, namely, the Stoic concept of freedom.[7] For the Stoic, freedom is "the greatest good" (Epictetus Diss. IV, 9,52; Dio Chrysostomus, Or. 14,1). Freedom unfolds itself when first the Stoic strives for independence from earthly treasures and enjoyments; he strives for frugality. Therefore, he must come to an inner imperturbability in the face of need and suffering. Epictetus describes this freedom from passions in this way: "Now nothing evil can happen to me; there are for me no robbers, no earthquakes, all is filled with peace, filled with tranquility" (Diss. III, 13,13). Finally, the resignation of the passions, apathy, is part of this concept. The Stoic frees himself from anger, hate, vengeance, rage, but also from compassion, from admiration and even more, from the fear of death.

The border line of apathy shows immediately how remote this philosophical ideal is from the religious concept of freedom. The philosophical position becomes unnatural, while the religious one keeps reality in sight, although the Christian knows the transcendence of his existence. The Christian does not suffocate the senses and passions. He accepts suffering, but only in the belief that it belongs to the world and that God will one day give him glory. It sounds paradoxical: worldly Stoic freedom misses our existence in the world, while supernatural Christian freedom grasps

[7] Cf. A. Bonhöffer, *Epiktet und das Neue Testament* (Gießen, 1911); O. Schmitz, *Der Freiheitsgedanke bei Epiktet und das Freiheitszeugnis bei Paulus* (Gütersloh, 1923); M. Müller, "Freiheit," *ZNW* 25 (1926) 177-236, especially 179-192; H. Schlier, Über das vollkommene Gesetz. . . ."

and overcomes it. Sometimes the Stoic himself became conscious that a complete extermination of passions was impossible, and that conquering the fear of death was unsuccessful. Epictetus, the academic teacher of idealistic youth, once said,

Show me one who is sick and is still happy, one who is in danger and is still happy, one who lies dying and is still happy, one who is cursed and is still happy, show me him! I have demanded to see a Stoic. But you can show me none who represents him perfectly, therefore show me one at least who is on the path, who is striving in this direction! Give me this comfort; do not begrudge an old man the marvel that I have not yet seen! (Diss. II, 19, 24f.).

We would like to take the elderly Epictetus by the hand and lead him to Paul, who would answer, "We are treated . . . as unknown and yet well known; as dying and behold, we live; as punished and yet not killed; as sorrowful, yet always rejoicing; as poor, yet making many rich; as having nothing and yet possessing everything" (2 Cor 6:9f.). This is the difficult and blessed existence the Apostle had experienced in this world, and such apostolic experience should be exemplary for every Christian. The reason is that he is unbroken by all suffering and trials. He is free and happy. He does not rely upon a philosophical or ethical training but upon that faith which overcomes the world—"Even though our outer man is wasting away, yet our inner man is being renewed day by day. For this slight momentary affliction is preparing for us an eternal weight of glory beyond all comparison, because we look not to the things that are seen but to the things that are unseen" (2 Cor 4:17f.). We need add nothing to this; these are not words about the inner freedom, but rather the witness of a free man. Paul, who is a Christian exhausted by want and war, reveals the existential greatness of Christian freedom.

CHAPTER V

The "New Man" According to Paul

If one can make the representation of man a test for a "Weltanschauung," then the Bible's representation of man, particularly in the New Testament, becomes the center of the Christian understanding of the world. Holy Scripture explicitly relates the world, or "creation," to man. "For the creation was subjected to futility, not of its own will but by the will of him who subjected it in hope; because the creation itself will be set free from its bondage to decay and obtain the glorious liberty of the children of God" (Rom 8:20f.). This anthropocentric view of the world may be difficult for modern, scientifically thinking man. Therefore we do not want to begin with the world as "creation" and to relate it to man and human history. Rather we shall consider man as the New Testament sees him in his Christian existence, that is, as a historical being in this world, and ask how the world in which man lives and

81

works represents itself as his world. After correlating man and world, we shall attempt to formulate a Christian notion of the world. The text from Colossians (3:9-11) offers an excellent guide: "Do not lie to one another, seeing that you have put off the old man with his practices and have put on the new man who is being renewed in knowledge after the image of his creator. Here there cannot be Greek and Jew, circumcised and uncircumcised, Barbarian and Scythian, slave and free man, but Christ is all, and in all."

1   CREATION AND PRESENT REALITY

We often draw from the New Testament a negative and pessimistic idea of the world: The world is treated as an enemy of God, an area that has become a slave to evil, filled with corrupt tendencies and lust (1 Jn 2:15ff.). It passes away and is doomed to destruction (1 Cor 7:31), so that friendship with the world is hostility toward God (Jas 4:4). Such a dualistically colored view of "this world" and "this age," which was influenced by contemporary intellectual currents of thought (Apocalyptic, Gnosis), actually dominates the language of New Testament authors.[1] One often overlooks, first, the intention of the statements, which in

[1] For the notion of "world" in the New Testament see R. Loewe, *Kosmos und Aion* (Gütersloh, 1935); H. Sasse, κόσμος," *ThWNT* 3 (1939) 882-896; J. M. Robinson, "The Biblical View of the World," *Encounter* 20 (1959) 470-483; R. Völkl, *Christ und Welt nach dem Neuen Testament* (Würzburg, 1960), with bibliography; R. Schnackenburg, *Die Johannesbriefe*, rev. ed. (Freiburg, 1962) 133-137; W. Schrage, "Die Stellung zur Welt bei Paulus, Epiktet und in der Apokalyptik," *Zeitschrift für Theologie und Kirche* 61 ((1964) 125-154.

these texts is directed toward the moral admonition not to make oneself "conformed to this world" (Rom 12:2). In these passages the world is not judged as God's creation, but as a sphere of man's conduct. Second, one overlooks that the Bible considers the world in the temporal dimension.[2] It does not treat of its natural evolution, but of its "history" as it is made by man. This latter was the pernicious development. Third, one overlooks the historical limitations of the authors, who emphasize the dark and ominous aspects of life and are caught in the intellectual current characteristic of their time.[3] Finally, one overlooks the eschatological mood of early Christianity, that of apprehensive expectation, which as such does not belong essentially to the Christian faith, but must be understood from the contemporary situation.

In view of the "new man" which is depicted in Colos-

[2] It is important that in Hebrew there is only one expression for "world" which means its temporal dimension ('olam), and a similar one for the spatial category is lacking. In order to denote the "universe" Hebrew uses the transcription "the heavens and the earth" (Gen 1:1, etc.) or "all" (Ps 8:7; Is 44:24 et al.). Cf. article by H. Sasse (see note above) 880.

[3] This "dualistic" view and pessimistic feeling were predominant in all intellectual areas of that time and also characteristic of the later Judaism. Cf. W. Bousset and H. Gressmann, Die Religion des Judentums im späthellenistischen Zeitalter, 3rd ed. (Tübingen, 1926) 251-254, 331-342; G. F. Moore, Judaism, vol. 1 (Cambridge, 1927) 445-459; H. Jonas, Gnosis und spätantiker Geist, vol. 1 (Göttingen, 1934); S. Pétrement, Le dualisme chez Platon, les gnostiques et les manichéens (Paris, 1947); U. Bianchi, Il dualismo religioso (Rome, 1958); J. Duchesne-Guillemin and H. Dörrie, "Dualismus," Reallexikon für Antike und Christentum, vol. 4 (Stuttgart, 1959) 334-350. For the Qumran-texts where this dualism is particularly noticeable see H. W. Huppenbauer, Der Mensch zwischen zwei Welten (Zürich, 1959).

sians 3:10, our thought focuses on the original creation, reminding us that man was created according to the "image and likeness" of God (Gen 1:26f.). The priestly codex places the creation of man after the rest of creation as the final and highest act. The other creatures are, as it were, summed up in him, but at the same time man surpasses all creatures because of his likeness to God. Therefore, all of creation is elevated and drawn closer to God through man, as God conceived and created him. The likeness of man with God may be difficult to describe,[4] but one thing is clear: man receives all creation that he might participate in God's sovereignty. Man, belonging to the world of creation, surpasses and governs it, thus bestowing upon it a splendor that is a reflection of God. Since the culmination of creation in man draws creation nearer to God and binds it more closely to him, the creation of man "according to God's image and likeness," as it is alluded to in Colossians 3:10, confirms the essential goodness of creation and its relationship with God. This knowledge of the goodness of the world created by God is never lost in the Bible, even when the New Testament speaks of "this age" and considers this

[4] Cf. D. Cairns, *The Image of God in Man* (New York, London, 1953); J. J. Stamm, *Die Gottebenbildlichkeit des Menschen im Alten Testament* (Zürich, 1959); J. Jervell, *Imago Dei. Gen 1, 26f im Spätjudentum, in der Gnosis und bei Paulus* (Göttingen, 1960); G. C. Berkouwer, *Man, the Image of God* (Grand Rapids, 1962); G. Söhngen, "Die biblische Lehre von der Gottebenbildlichkeit des Menschen," *Pro Veritate*, Festgabe für L. Jaeger und W. Stählin (Münster i.W. und Kassel, 1963) 23-57; H. Wildberger, Das Ebenbild Gottes, Gen 1, 26-30," *Theologische Zeitschrift* 21 (1965) 245-259, 481-501.

present world, which we experience, as evil and filled
with suffering.

Both notions of the world—positive and negative—
are not separated from each other. This becomes clear
if we consider man in his present state. Although he
continues to be the image of God, he experiences himself as a being inclined to evil. This is expressed by the
"old man." As man now finds himself in his earthly
existence, he is a terrifying vision of evil inclinations
and sinful desires. A whole catalogue of vices can be
enumerated, "Immorality, impurity, passion, evil desire and covetousness (v. 5) . . . anger, wrath, malice,
slander, and foul talk from your mouth (v. 8)." If the
natural man consists of such evil instincts, though he
is capable of good actions, the destructive tendency
of his nature remains a sinister reality that justifies and
makes understandable the negative evaluation of the
world.[5] Considered honestly and objectively the world
as the sphere of historical action must appear to man
in the same way that he experiences himself. The Bible,
with its tradition of the fall of man, comprehends and
preserves a primitive knowledge of man's nature,
which is represented in the paradise narrative as a

[5] For the biblical view of "man," in general, see G. v. Rad, H.
Schlier *et. al.*, *Der alte und der neue Mensch* (München, 1942);
K. Galling, *Das Bild des Menschen in biblischer Sicht* (Mainz,
1947); C. R. Smith, *The Biblical Doctrine of Man* (London,
1951); C. H. Dodd, P. I. Bratsiotis, R. Bultmann, and H. Clavier,
Man in God's Design (Newcastle, 1952); G. E. Wright, *The Bib-
lical Doctrine of Man in Society* (London, 1954); H. Lamparter,
Das biblische Menschenbild (Stuttgart, 1956); A. Gelin,
L'homme selon la Bible (Paris, 1962); L. Scheffczyk, *Der mod-
erne Mensch vor dem biblischen Menschenbild* (Freiburg, 1964).

"myth"—a myth nevertheless that contains profound truth (Gen 2-3). Man is fallen from God and has exchanged "the glory of the incorruptible God" for the image according to corruptible men (Rom 1:23). "Therefore God gave them up in the lusts of their hearts to impurity, to the dishonoring of their bodies among themselves, because they exchanged the truth about God for a lie and worshiped and served the creature rather than the creator. . ." (Rom 1:24f.).

It is a peculiar phenomenon of the Old Testament[6] that the idea of man created in the image and likeness of God is maintained in spite of man's sinful self-idolization in subsequent history. After the fall of man the likeness to God given in creation is not lost. The "genealogy of Adam," with which the history of human generation begins, explicitly calls to mind this fact (Gen 5:1f.). God gives to Noe and his sons the blessing of creation after the flood, and he establishes again the dignity of man "according to his image" (Gen 9:1-7). Psalm 8 praises God who crowned man "with splendor and glory" (v. 6). But another passage states, "The instinct of the human heart is inclined to evil from youth" (Gen 8:21). This truth is verified throughout the history of Israel, even in the conduct of the

[6] For the view of man in the Old Testament see J. Hempel, *Gott und Mensch im Alten Testament*, 2nd ed. (Stuttgart, 1936); W. Eichrodt, *Das Menschenverständnis des Alten Testaments*, 2nd ed. (Zürich, 1947); W. Whitefield, *God and Man in the Old Testament* (London, 1949); W. Zimmerli, *Das Menschenbild im Alten Testament* (München, 1949); P. Pidoux, *L'homme dans l'Ancien Testament* (Neuchâtel, Paris, 1953); A.-M. Dubarle, "La conception de l'homme dans l'Ancien Testament," *Sacra Pagina*, vol. 1 (Gembloux, 1959) 522-536; G. v. Rad, *Theologie des Alten Testaments*, vol 2 (München, 1960) 359-364.

pious and just. The two aspects of the religious notion of the world, the goodness and glory of creation and the historical perversion and corruption, cannot be more clearly and realistically expressed than in this view of man.

This primitive knowledge and this intense experience have also entered into the baptismal exhortation of the epistle to the Colossians (3). The Apostle does not directly reflect upon the creation narrative and the likeness of man to God. He does not keep directly before his eyes the entire history of mankind which is under the curse of sin, but he views man in his naked existence and historical situation.[7] Man always bears the image of his creator, but only in the distorted reflection of his ungodlike conduct and action. Paul emphasizes this behavior of the worldly man, the "old man" (v. 9): through his actions he is alienated from God. He no longer knows his creator and he therefore does not know himself, his dignity, or his glory. Because the Bible thinks "anthropocentrically," it is by anthropocentric thinking that we find the key to its notion of the world.

The created world was subjected to "futility" or "vanity" ($\mu\alpha\tau\alpha\iota\acute{o}\tau\eta s$ [Rom 8:20]). This is a term that sounds moral: it is a vain, ineffective striving condemned to

[7] For the view of man in the New Testament see W. G. Kümmel, *Das Bild des Menschen im Neuen Testament* (Zürich, 1948); H. Mehl-Koehnlein, *L'homme selon l'apôtre Paul* (Neuchâtel, Paris, 1951); D. W. Stacey, *The Pauline View of Man* (London, 1956); R. Bultmann, "Das Verständnis von Welt und Mensch im Neuen Testament und im Griechentum," *Glauben und Verstehen*, vol 2 (Tübingen, 1952) 59-78; C. Spicq, *Dieu et l'homme selon le Nouveau Testament* (Paris, 1961); L. Cerfaux, *Le chrétien dans la théologie paulinienne* (Paris, 1962).

failure, an attempt at self-existence leading directly to
self-annihilation (1 Cor 3:20; Eph 4:17; Acts 14:15).
It actually means the frailty and transitoriness of the
creature ($\phi\theta o\rho\acute{a}$ [v. 21]), but this instability appears
more as a moral quality than an essential quality. It
does not simply say that creation was freed from the
curse, but creation was freed from the "bondage" or
"slavery" of the curse (v. 21).[8] Existence itself does not
appear to have changed, but the "character" of creation—its experiential situation—has changed. According to the Apostle's understanding, we might say:
creation, through man's fall from God, has been torn
away from its relation with the creator and has lost its
deep significance. Therefore, it groans and sighs in the
present situation, waiting impatiently and hoping im-
petuously for its future liberation.

Basically the Bible reveals the relation of the world to
man and the effect of his moral conduct on the world.
Since man through his moral guilt has turned his existential situation into evil, the rest of the world insofar
as it is "his" world, his sphere of existence, has been
drawn into corruption with him. The Bible in its unique
way makes this clear, when it uses human speech to
describe a creation that is nonrational. If the world is
to find salvation, then salvation must be inaugurated
by man.

II   RENEWAL OF MAN AND OF THE WORLD

Christian faith does not come to terms with the "old
man" and the existing conditions of the world. The

[8] See chap. 4 in this book (note 6).

coming of a new man and of a new world belong to the central message of faith. The doctrine of the "new heaven and new earth" (Ap 21:1-5) is frequently understood as an apocalyptic event having no relation to us because of our scientific way of thinking. The modern man looks critically and skeptically upon such religious promises. In his famous lecture, "The New Testament and Mythology," R. Bultmann says: "He who is convinced that the world which is known to us will end in the future imagines its end still as the result of a natural evolution, as a terminating in a natural catastrophe and not as the mythical event of which the New Testament speaks."[9] The decisive insight for the Christian faith, however, is not when and how this world will end, but that it cannot in its present form be final. In its need and suffering it cries out for a new form. This idea is in some way emphasized by all human envisioning of the future. That man might endure the present world, as he experiences it with its enigma and obscurity, and in order that he might overcome the future, he conceives a vision of an idealistic end that corresponds to his "Weltanschauung." Christian faith is a genuine answer to the question engaging all men: How will the world survive in the future and how will man attain his salvation? The decisive impulse for our mentality toward the present world proceeds from our view of the future. Christian faith foresees a transfigured world created anew through the power of God. It is not a mere fantasy, for it is founded on the conviction of man's present renewal.

[9] See this lecture in *Kerygma und Mythos*, vol. 1 ed. H. W. Bartsch (Hamburg, 1948) 15-53, especially 19.

The text from Colossians (3:9-11) emphasizes the "new man" as opposed to the "old man." This "new man" is not a vague image in the mind of the believer —but rather a reality.[10] The coming world of glory is revealed in this "new man" and yet the very same man conceals this revelation. The text is a baptismal exhortation, which refers to the mysterious divine event in baptism, and from this draws conclusions. The participle (ἀπεκδυσάμενοι) attached to the imperative "Do not lie to one another" can be understood in different ways. It could be a continuation of the admonition, or, since it would not appear in the past form without good reason, it probably should be interpreted as an indicative referring to the baptismal event ("seeing that you have put off"). In the final analysis both questions are irrelevant, since the paragraph in either case presupposes the statements concerning our salvation (Col 2): by circumcision performed "without hands" (that is, "the circumcision of Christ") we were buried with Christ in baptism, in which we were also raised with him (v. 12). We possess in Christ a new life, hidden with him in God (3:3), but which will appear in glory (3:4). This hidden reality, grasped only in faith, urges us to form a new external life and becomes a powerful moral challenge in this world. Both aspects—the grace-giving event that happens to us and the moral appeal arising from it—are equally emphasized. With the "old man" and his deeds we should take off and put to death

[10] Cf. W. Matthias, "Der alte und der neue Mensch in der Anthropologie des Paulus," *Evangelische Theologie* 17 (1957) 385-397; B. Rey, "L'homme nouveau d'après S. Paul," *Revue des Sciences Philos. et Théolog.* 48 (1964) 603-629, also 49 (1965) 161-195.

the bad inclinations in us, the evil passions ruling us
(3:5ff.). We have put on the "new man" who is being
renewed according to the image of his creator, but it
is a renewal "in knowledge," in moral trial, in a matur-
ing relationship with God, so that the admonition unfolds: "Put on then, as God's chosen ones, holy and be-
loved, compassion, kindness, lowliness, meekness, and
patience . . ." (3:12ff.).

In summing up the aspects that are standard for the
"new man," and that elucidate the Christian understanding of the world, there is, first, the grace of the
hidden renewal, which comes to us from God. Second,
there is included in it the hope for future fulfillment.
This is not an empty and unfounded expectation, but
one based upon faith in the risen Christ, who is the
first-born from the dead (Col 1:18). Finally, there is
the moral renewal that makes possible with the help
of God a new way of life, a new conduct transforming
man and human society. All these aspects are inextrica-
bly bound together and overlap each other in man's
world.[11] Therefore, a new form arises for the existing
world that man historically experiences. The new crea-

[11] For the relationship between sacrament, ethics, and eschatology in the thought of Paul see H. v. Soden, *Sakrament und Ethik
bei Paulus* (Gotha, 1931); S. Djukanovič, *Heiligkeit und Heili-
gung bei Paulus* (Novi Sad, 1939); A. Kirchgässner, *Erlösung
und Sünde* 147-157; G. Bornkamm, *Das Ende des Gesetzes* 34-
50; Ch. Haufe, *Die sittliche Rechtfertigungslehre des Paulus*
(Halle, 1957); R. Bultmann, *Theologie des Nuen Testaments*, 3rd
ed. (Tübingen, 1958) 332-341; E. Larsson, *Christus als Vorbild*
(Uppsala, 1962); L. Cerfaux, *Le chrétien* 288-302, 406-426; R.
Schnackenburg, *Baptism in the Thought of St. Paul* (Oxford,
1964) 187-203; *The Moral Teaching of the New Testament* (New
York, 1965) 268-286.

tion of man is more clearly described in the parallel passage (Eph 4:24): the *new man* is "created after the likeness of God in true righteousness and holiness." This is a fundamental affirmation of the order of creation. But this idea is possible through the hope of a future new creation, which will be a restoration (cf. ἀποκατάστασις [Acts 3:21]), a "new birth" (cf. παλιγγενεσία [Mt 19:28]) of the original godlike world. It will not be a destruction but rather a consummation of the first creation. Faith in the eschatological perfection bestows upon the first creation its full excellence. Just as man in the past was God's steward and the administrator of the created world, the "new man in the present should be the same for the renewal of his own humanity; he is therefore called a "new creation" in Christ (2 Cor 5:17).

The concept of "renewal" conveys the eschatological aspect of the new creation. The declaration of the "renewal," however, forces us to examine that new creation. In the end God will say, "Behold I make all things new" (καινά [Ap 21:5]). What God gives to the Chrision is a present anticipation of the future. It takes place in the fundamental act of baptism ("the washing of regeneration and renewal in the Holy Spirit" (Tit 3:5), but retains also its effect and power (present), internally strengthening and regenerating the "new man" in daily life (2 Cor 4:16). It also works toward the renewal of our mind (Rom 12:2). In the passage quoted above, Paul formulates the idea more tersely and precisely, "If any one is in Christ, he is a new creation; the old has passed away, behold, the new has come" (2 Cor 5:17; Gal 6:15). What the entire world will ex-

perience happens to a man who in faith and in baptism
is already united with God; he attains in Christ a new
existence that has an eschatological nature. Life, therefore, appears in the midst of this present age, which is
a future life, and it gains power over man who through
and in Christ has become a "new creation."

At the same time a further element comes to light,
which in the epistle to the Colossians is not so clearly
expressed: the "new man" is a man formed in *Christ*.
Only with difficulty can one directly apply to Christ
the expression "according to the image of the creator,"
although in another passage he is called "the image of
the invisible God" (Col 1:15; 2 Cor 4:4). Pauline theology affirms that the idea is adapted to Christ, the first-
born to the life of future glory (1 Cor 15:22). Christ
is the Second Adam, the "man of heaven," whose image
we should bear, just as we have carried the image of the
first Adam, the "man of dust" (1 Cor 15:49). God also
predestined us to be "conformed to the image of his
Son," in which we are united with him (Rom 8:29; Phil
3:21). Beholding the glory of the Lord, with unveiled
face, we are being changed into his likeness from one
degree of glory to another (2 Cor 3:18). The expression
"put on the new man" (Gal 3:27) becomes the other
parallel "put on Christ." That the "new man" is one
elevated by Christ, one formed in him, a man filled
with his life and nature, is evident from Colossians
3:11. Our fulfillment in Christ is established here not
individually, but collectively for all who are united
through Christ to a new community: "Christ is all and
in all." The Christian thus has a clear goal in his aspiration to be a "new man": Christ the resurrected,

clothed in his transfigured body, who has entered into the glory of God. The whole man, "flesh" and "body," is included in this process, which with the resurrection attains its final consummation.

This is and remains a mystery of faith, which only he who believes in the resurrection of Jesus from the dead can affirm. The actual new creation remains hidden in the present age, and the real "transfiguration" remains reserved for the future world. But the immediate need of the present is moral renewal.

We will once again consider the moral aspect. Any enthusiastic attempt to project the glory of the perfected man (and the future world) into the present world is hindered by a severe moral imperative. It takes as its basis the previous world with its trials and needs. The Christian must first "suffer with Christ in order that we may also be glorified with him" (Rom 8:17). Just as the baptismal exhortation gives the admonition "not to lie to one another," Paul also warns us against a self-deception that might let the Christian think himself to be above temptation and fall. "Let anyone who thinks that he stands take heed lest he fall" (1 Cor 10:12). In Corinth there were fanatics who thought themselves to be "already perfect" because of their spiritual experiences (1 Cor 2:6). Paul attacked their self-centered boasting with the description of the wretched existence of Christ's apostles: "Already you are filled! Already you have become rich! Without us you have become kings! And would that you did reign, so that we might share the rule with you! For I think that God has exhibited us apostles as last of all, like men sentenced to death ..." (1 Cor 4:8f.). The Christian must be realistic and open his eyes to both things, the continuing moral struggle and the necessity of suffering. The existential situation of the Christian, who stands in the world but endures it with the power of God, is described well in the words of the Apostle: "For though we live in the world we are not carrying on a worldly war, for the weapons of our warfare are not worldly, but have divine power to destroy strongholds" (2 Cor 10:3f.). The powers of the future world do not break out openly and perceptibly but are hidden. At most they are capable of being perceived in faith and in the moral struggle of the new man who is formed by Christ and grows in the likeness of God. For man, who is responsible for the moral decline and the historical deterioration of the world, salvation itself must begin in the old world with its needs and obscurities. Man is the starting point for the renewal of our existing world. The battle of man, the "new man," must be fought as long as this world lasts. With the transfiguration of man at the end of the world, the new creation of God, a transfigured world, will emerge.

III   THE NEW HUMAN RACE

The passage with which we are concerned (Col 3:9-11) contains another statement that is important for our understanding of man and the world: with the "new man" there comes into existence also a new community, where "there cannot be Greek and Jew, circumcised, barbarian, Scythian, slave, free man, but Christ is all and in all" (v. 11). Two additional passages with similar negative enumerations (Gal 3:28; 1 Cor 12:13) confirm that baptism is the place where the previous natural differences disappear. In Galatians it also says that the sexual differences (man and woman) are abolished, because all are one in Christ. This can be easily misunderstood, so that the Christian appears to have no more sense of the fundamental sexual differences which lie in the created order itself (Gen 1:27). The Pauline idea refers only to the new order of redeemed mankind, our being "in Christ," and it is therefore a foreshadowing of the final consummation. It is not so much a recourse to the original creation as it is a preview of the new creation that is to come, which exceeds and perfects the first creation. The future world will certainly retain the features of the present, but the transfiguration will banish all sorrow, want, and pain (Ap 21:4). Insofar as the worldly differences—national, religious, social, cultural, and sexual—lead to conflict, they will become ineffective; the previous sorrowful history of man will come to an end. The transfiguration of the body, the glory of God exalting the entire new creation and its life, will abolish all earthly conflict and involvements in our earthly life. All enmity between nations, social inequality, differences in language, and similar things will cease; all will stand in the light of God (Ap 21:23f., 22:4f.).

The expression which is perhaps already a formula, "Christ is all and in all," makes clear that the unity of previously conflicting elements is realized in the sphere of Christ's influence and dominion. The entire new collectivity ("all") represents Christ, who appears as a corporate personality: all are "the one" in Christ Jesus

(Gal 3:28).[12] This (collective) Christ is one body, which has many members and yet is still a single body (1 Cor 12:12). It is the body of Christ (1 Cor 12:27), the body which after Christ's resurrection is constituted by the Spirit, or as we could also say, "a single body in Christ" (Rom 12:5). This is a peculiar conception: this new human community which is constituted "in Christ" cannot be considered close enough with Christ. The second part of the formula "and Christ is in all" is important for the understanding of the first part "Christ is all." In all these men who differ in their very origin and earthly type, Christ is present and operative. Insofar as they stand in the sphere of his dominion, they have become a unity, and their previous differences disappear.

Instead of pursuing these notions that raise special problems for theologians,[13] it might be well to find

[12] Cf. H. Wheeler Robinson, "The Hebrew Conception of Corporate Personality," *Zeitschrift für die alttestamentliche Wissenschaft, Beiheft* 66 (1936) 49-61; S. Hanson, *The Unity of the Church in the New Testament* (Uppsala, 1946); L. S. Thornton, *The Common Life in the Body of Christ*, 3rd ed. (London, 1950); E. Best, *One Body in Christ* (London, 1955), who clearly develops the basic idea of "corporate personality" for the Pauline notion; B. J. Le Frois, "Semitic Totality Thinking," *CBQ* 17 (1955) 315-323; R. Schnackenburg, *Baptism* 112-121; J. de Fraine, *Adam et son lignage* (Bruges, 1959).

[13] For the discussion concerning the "In Christ"-formula and the concept of the "Body of Christ" see W. Grossouw, *In Christ* (Westminster, 1952); A. Wikenhauser, *Die Christusmystik des Apostels Paulus*, rev. ed. (Freiburg, 1956); F. Neugebauer, *In Christus* (Göttingen, 1961); M. Bouttier, *En Christ* (Paris, 1962); J. A. T. Robinson, *The Body* (London, 1952); E. Schweizer, "Die Kirche als Leib Christi . . .", *Theologische Literaturzeitung 86* (1961), col. 161-174, 241-256; J. J. Meuzelaar, *Der Leib des*

what this image of the new human race in Christ signifies for the Christian understanding of the world. In his world man conceives himself in a peculiar tension, which is both individual and social. Each conception must provide a solution to the relation between individual and community: in the East the socialistic man is absorbed by the community; in the West the freely developing personality is limited as little as possible by social institutions. In both conceptions the relation is unsatisfactorily solved—one can say unsolved. According to the order of creation the Christian man is seen in personal dignity as the "image and likeness of God," and this is affirmed in the new creation. But the social relationship of man is not overlooked. In the Old Testament it appears in the unity of the individual with "natural" communities of family and clan, tribe and folk, which is understandable among Semites and Orientals. Therefore, one can speak of a "collective" way of thinking. The narrowness arising from this outlook is overcome in the New Testament by the universal inclusion of the entire human race in the redemption-event. The individual is not only placed in a free area of individual activities but is also strongly bound to and deeply rooted in this new community of the redeemed. He who "in Christ" has become a "new creation," becomes at the same time a member of a new community: "You are all one in Christ Jesus (Gal 3:28).

Messias (Neukirchen, 1961); J. Havet, "La doctrine paulinienne du 'Corps du Christ' ", *Recherches bibliques* 5 (Louvain, 1960) 185-216; R. Schnackenburg, *Die Kirche im Neuen Testament* (Freiburg, 1961) 146-156, and American ed. *The Church in the New Testament* (New York, 1965); *The Church as the Body of Christ*, with various contributions (Notre Dame, 1963).

A Christian cannot free himself from the obligation of Christ's community. The unity of all is nowhere more strongly expressed than in the idea of the "body of Christ." This "builds itself up in love" (Eph 4:16), and the law of love and harmony is imposed on all who are "members one of another" (Eph 4:25). It becomes explicit in the admonition to brotherly love (Col 3:12ff.). This new community of the redeemed is also "open" for the entire human race, and it is its task in the world, through the power of its faith and the witness of its love, to call and incorporate all men into the community of Christ (Eph 3:9f., 4:15 f.).

The Christian idea of a "new human race" is more fundamental and more comprehensive than the ideas of worldly ideologies. A new human race remains as the goal of the new man, which will be realized in the future, in the new world that originates from God. But the uniting force of that perfect community, namely, love, can and should even now mitigate and overcome the present tensions and struggles. Love, which has its deepest source in the one triune God, becomes an eschatological force in the midst of the present world. Hence, this passage from Colossians reveals the basic Christian view of the world reflected in the Christian image of man. It deals with man and his existence in this world. It brings the Christian closer to an understanding of himself and the community to which he belongs. Therefore, he gains an insight into the world wherein he lives and operates. The world is seen in its historical reality, but through faith it is placed in the perspective of creation and new creation. With a glimpse into the future the original creation rises in its pure divine splendor, which it has never lost but which has been tarnished by man and his deeds. The new creation, which will restore and surpass the splendor of the first creation, begins in man. Human history, which litigates against salvation, has through the coming of the Son of God become again a history of salvation. Christ, the image of the invisible God, in his role of the resurrected and transfigured, becomes the goal of the redeemed man and the head of the redeemed human race. In Christ the future is already present and effective; in him those bound to him participate in the life of the future world but remain also citizens of the historical world, which they should penetrate with the power of faith and love until God makes all things new.

CHAPTER VI

Dying and Rising with Christ: A Pauline Notion

Our existence in the world is constantly threatened by sorrow, privation, and death, as well as darkened by sin and guilt. Religion reveals its power to overcome the desolation and darkness of human life. And Christian faith is especially efficacious in this direction, for Christ himself trod the way through death to glory. In the Pauline epistles we see exactly how profoundly the Apostle grasped, theologically penetrated, and personally applied this revelation of God in Christ to his life. The Pauline notion of dying and rising with Christ is a principle that possesses great value for Christian existence in general. Although we meet related expressions in most of Paul's epistles, we properly understand this Pauline notion only when we carefully study the passage on baptism found in Romans 6:1-11. Proceeding from this point, and thus from the basic concept of sacramental "dying and rising with Christ," we shall concentrate on broader statements proving that this notion is a central theme in the whole of Pauline thought—one that penetrates his personal life and becomes as well a model for every Christian's existence.

I   DYING AND RISING WITH CHRIST IN BAPTISM

It is hardly possible to treat exhaustively Paul's well-known text on baptism (Rom 6:1-11), which is filled with many exegetical problems. We can only discuss the most important parts and attempt a more accurate translation: "Do you not know that all of us who have been baptized into Christ Jesus were baptized into his death? We were buried therefore with him by baptism into death, so that as Christ was raised from the dead by the glory of the Father, we too might walk in newness of life. For if we have grown together with the likeness of his death, we shall certainly grow together with that of the resurrection. We know that our old man was crucified with him so that the body of sin might be destroyed, and we might no longer be enslaved to sin. But if we have died with Christ, we believe that we shall also live with him."

We shall try to steer away from the interpretations of other scholars and simply present our own explanations in a positive way.[1] In this context the Apostle refutes an objection to his teaching on grace. In the preceding chapter of Romans (5:12-21), Paul teaches that, because God's grace would abound with the coming of

---

[1] For a fuller discussion see R. Schnackenburg, *Baptism in the Thought of St. Paul* (Oxford, 1964); American ed. (New York, 1964).

Christ and because it would by far surpass the damage wrought for mankind by Adam, less prudent men might conclude: "Let us remain in sin, so that grace might abound!" (6:1). Paul rejects this false and dangerous conclusion with the objection that we have once and for all died to sin and are committed to a new life for God in Christ. In order to reinforce his argument, Paul refers to baptism and invests it with a new and deeper interpretation. His readers know that they have been baptized into Christ and now belong entirely to him. Paul, however, remarks even more clearly that in baptism they have been baptized into the death of Christ and that they have died to the malice of sin. In this connection he always understands sin to be a power that formerly dominated us, a power to which we have died through this baptism unto death and which we have completely thrown off.

The Apostle probably refers to the symbolism of baptism as it was then administered: a person was totally submerged in water so that he disappeared in it. But this liturgical symbolism represents a much more profound reality, namely, that we are incorporated into the death of Christ, who died definitively to the power of sin for all of us. We recognize this return to Christ's death when Paul in verse 6 remarks unexpectedly, "Our old man was *crucified* with him," that is, with Christ. Hence, when we disappear under the water's surface in baptism, it symbolizes a mystical union with the death and burial of Christ. Along with the external event occurs an interior event with consequences for our salvation: we are crucified with Christ so that our "old man," who was a slave to sin, is destroyed. Moreover, we also know by faith that Christ did not remain in the grip of death but was raised from the dead by the power of the Father. "The death he died, he died to sin, once for all, but the life he lives, he lives to God," Paul remarks in verse 10. Thus, we also die with him, that with him we might live to God. That is the meaning of the "newness of life" in which we should walk. This passage refers primarily to our moral life but involves more than simply a moral attitude. There is an actual participation in the life of the risen Christ. This has begun for us in baptism and will reach its final perfection only at the moment of our own resurrection. This eschatological perspective is revealed in verse 8, "But if we have died with Christ, we believe that we shall also live with him."

Up to this point everything should be clear. It is more difficult, however, to grasp the nature of this union initiated in baptism, by which we enter into the death and resurrection of Christ and so with Christ himself are crucified and raised from the dead. In verse 5 we come across a mode of expression that is concise and difficult to translate: "For if we have grown together with the likeness of his death, we shall certainly grow together with that of the resurrection." The Apostle obviously wants to express the whole reality of the event, of our actual union in the death and resurrection of Christ. To "have grown together" is a vivid image for a close union. The Vulgate in this instance did not translate "complantati" accurately enough, that is, to "have been planted together." The Greek version is even more arresting: We have been drawn entirely into Christ's death so that we ourselves

have died with Christ, and with him have been crucified. This lays the foundation for solving the difficulties involved in our consideration of just how we can
"grow together and share in the likeness of the long
past death of Christ on the cross.

This is best explained by noting that Paul had previously developed the typology of Adam and Christ
(5:12-23), and regards Christ not only as an individual,
but also as head or progenitor of the whole of a new
mankind, namely, of all who believe in him. Now, according to Semitic thought, the progenitor represents
the whole of those followers or that posterity united
with him, so that he acts on behalf of all who are still
to come and who share in his destiny.[2] Thus, Paul
states: "Since one died for all, therefore all died (2 Cor
5:14). Through baptism we have been included in the
destiny of our spiritual progenitor, Christ. We have
undergone the same thing he has, and we have done
so in union with him. Not only does our Christian faith
witness "that Christ died for our sins according to the
scriptures, and that he was buried and that he rose
again on the third day according to the scriptures . . ."
(1 Cor 15:3f.), but also all who believe in him, all who
have been baptized unto his name and who thus belong to him testify to it. We, too, have died with Christ,
have been buried with him, so that we might also rise
with him. Baptism is the saving event allotted to each
one of us, which at the same time unites us to the community of Christ, wherein we receive new being "in
Christ" (ἐν Χριστῷ). The Apostle clearly indicates this
at the end of the passage in Romans, "So you also must

[2] Cf. previous chapter on the "new man," note 12.

consider yourselves dead to sin and alive to God in Christ Jesus" (6:11).

In Colossians we find the same thought expressed, namely, that in baptism a sacramental, actual dying and rising occurs: "In Christ you have been circumcised with a circumcision made without hands, by putting off the body of the flesh in the circumcision of Christ, and you were buried with him in baptism. In him you were also raised through faith in the working of God who raised him from the dead. . . ." (2:11f.). But a comparison of Paul's thought in Romans and Colossians reveals a certain theological refinement: in Romans Paul says that as a consequence of our baptism we should lead a new life with Christ, and that we shall (one day) also live with him; but in Colossians Paul says that in baptism we have *already* been raised from the dead. This advancement in thought depends, most likely, upon the situation for which the epistle was intended. In Romans Paul's main consideration was the moral conclusion that since we no longer in any way belong to the power of sin, we *should* lead a new life. In Colossians Paul opposes a heresy by stressing that we have already obtained our salvation in Christ: now we already possess, at least in a hidden and preliminary way, the life of the risen Christ, or, as Paul himself says at the beginning of chapter 3, "You have died and your life is hid with Christ in God; when Christ, who is our life, appears, then you also will appear with him in glory." These are fine distinctions. In the earlier epistle the emphasis is laid upon "dying with Christ," and the future rising from the dead appears to be withheld, whereas in the later epistle this future hope is already more firmly anchored in the present. Objectively, the thought in both epistles hardly differs: there is already in baptism a "dying and rising with Christ," although our own bodily rising from the dead first happens at the end, on the last day.

Salvation has been bestowed upon us fundamentally and radically in baptism, a salvation in Christ and totally bound up with Christ. Our union with Christ, our sharing in his course and destiny, is most forcefully emphasized in these statements that constantly reiterate acting "with Christ." From the moment of baptism the Christian sees himself as a person crucified and raised from the dead with Christ. In this fundamental sacrament God himself has touched us with his grace. We will now consider how Paul draws far-reaching conclusions for the whole of our Christian existence.

II DYING AND RISING WITH CHRIST
IN OUR TEMPORAL CHRISTIAN EXISTENCE

Because the Christian is bound to Christ as closely as possible, Paul sees in our dying and rising with him a law or rule governing our whole Christian life.[3] This

[3] Cf. W. T. Hahn, *Das Mitsterben und Mitauferstehen mit Christus bei Paulus* (Gütersloh, 1937); P. Bonnard, "Mourir et vivre avec Jésus Christ selon s. Paul," *Rev. d'Hist. et de Philos. Relig.* 36 (1956) 101-112; O. Kuss, *Der Römerbrief* (Regensburg, 1957, 59) 329-381; A. Feuillet, "Mort du Christ et mort du chrétien d'après les épîtres pauliniennes," *RB* 66 (1959) 481-513; B. M. Ahern, "The Fellowship of His Sufferings," *CBQ* 22 (1960) 1-32; R. Schnackenburg, *Baptism* 139-177; L. Cerfaux, *Le chrétien dans la théologie paulinienne* (Paris, 1962) 302-306.

assimilation into the destiny of Jesus Christ, our Lord, is realized in a twofold manner: in the moral endeavors of the Christian and in his temporal condition.

1 Moral life as a dying to sin

In the epistle to the Galatians the Apostle remarks, "They who belong to Christ have crucified the flesh with its passions and desires" (5:24). The context is one where Paul underscores the necessity of decisive moral endeavor. He does not, however, simply enjoin an ethical imperative, but places this imperative within the new life of the spirit that has been given us: "If we live by the spirit, by the spirit let us also walk" (5:25). In the former he does not enjoin an imperative but says: "You *have* crucified the flesh." Finally, he turns his attention once again to baptism, in which our former self, bound to the service of sin, has been crucified with Christ. He means that just as our dying and rising has its origin in God, we *should* respond in our life by crucifying our flesh with Christ—or to phrase it even better, we should have crucified it for our whole lives. This same idea weaves its way throughout the whole of Pauline ethics: whatever you are, whatever you have become because of God's action, must be made a reality right now in your temporal existence. To paraphrase it more concisely, Paul places the moral imperative on the plane of the objective fact of grace.

But what does it mean "to crucify the flesh"? The Greek concept which we translate by the word "flesh" (σάρξ)[4], is difficult to explain. It does not mean simply

[4] Cf. W. Schauf, *Sarx* (Münster, 1924); W. G. Kümmel, *Römer*

the bodily aspect of man, or even in a more restricted
sense the sexual desires of man. It is much more comprehensive: the inclination toward sin of the whole
man on the temporal and bodily plane of existence; that
painful, destructive inclination we all experience.
Among the "carnal" desires Paul lists not only the
bodily or carnal instincts, but also those desires that we
would preferably designate as vices of the "spirit," for
example, dissension, anger, strife. Paul contrasts the
"carnal" man with the "spiritual" who is driven on
and led by the Spirit of God. "Walk by the Spirit, and
do not gratify the desires of the flesh. For the desires
of the flesh are against the Spirit, and the desires of the
Spirit are against the flesh; for these are opposed to
each other, to prevent you from doing what you would"
(Gal 5:16f.). Here, by "Spirit" is meant the divine,
Holy Spirit who from baptism fills us and moves us.
Thus, we also learn to recognize the unique character of
Christian morality, which takes up moral endeavor
because of God's strength and the Spirit of God who
has been bestowed upon us. We need do nothing more
than permit ourselves to be moved by the spirit of God,
and without resistance accept his promptings.

The fact is, however, that after baptism the Christian

7 und die Bekehrung des Paulus (Leipzig, 1929); C. H. Lindijer,
Het begrip Sarx bij Paulus (Assen, Netherlands, 1952); R. Bult-
mann, Theologie des Neuen Testaments 5th ed. (Tùbingen,
1965) 232-246; W D. Davies, "Paul and the Dead Sea Scrolls,
Flesh and Spirit," The Scrolls and the New Testament, ed. K.
Stendahl (New York, 1957) 157-182; R. E. Murphy, "Bsr in the
Qumrân Literature and Sarks in the Epistle to the Romans,
Sacra Pagina vol. 2 (Gembloux, 1959) 60-76; O. Kuss, Römer-
brief 506-540; E. Schweizer, "σαρξ," ThWNT 7 (1964) 124-138.

still finds himself living in his former body and is still exposed to temptations. Paul, employing the terminology of his time, speaks of "passions and desires." Contemporary man primarily understands "passions" to be strong emotional forces that can be employed for both good and evil. The Apostle, however, has in mind passions that impel man to sin. He sees man realistically, strikingly inclined toward evil acts, and he holds the power of sin accountable. Moral life is not without its battles, and so he readily employs corresponding images: "Let not sin therefore reign in your mortal bodies, to make you obey their passions. Do not yield your members to sin as instruments of wickedness, but yield yourselves to God as men who have been brought from death to life, and your members to God as instruments of righteousness" (Rom 6:12f.). Sin is seen as a power set upon war, which will imprison and enslave us, in order at the end to pay us our "soldier's wages" with eternal death (6:19f., 22). This power knows how to force its entry by means of desires and passions in us, it attracts us by using what is forbidden "you shall not covet," (7:7ff.), and it can gain the upper hand in us if we do not oppose it in the strength of the Holy Spirit.

The notion of dying and rising with Christ in our moral life also stands in the background of Colossians: "Mortify your members, which are on earth, immorality, impurity, passion, evil desire and covetousness . . ." (3:5). In a previous verse the Apostle mentioned that we have risen with Christ, and that we should seek the things that are above (v. 1). "Set your minds on things that are above, not on things that are on earth" (v. 2). Later, he resumes speaking about baptism, in which we have "set aside the old man with his deeds," in the way an old piece of clothing is set aside, and in which we "have put on the new man, who is being renewed in knowledge after the image of his Creator" (v. 9f.). There is, therefore, a moral "dying" and a moral "rising," which consists in having our home in heaven, in union with the risen Lord, and in the striving for the "things above." But in his admonitions the notions of "mortifying" and "crucifying" our old self with Christ assume greater importance. "Rising" and drawing near to Christ act more as a motive by which we persevere under the moral struggle that is necessary even at the present.

Thus, obsolete as it sounds, this admonition to "mortify our members" has a deeper and more positive meaning. We adhere to it only to commit ourselves to the crucified and risen Lord, in complete self-surrender to his person and destiny. It is not so much an ascetic training or struggle, but rather *a personal following and fellowship—the transposition of the discipleship of Jesus in his earthly life to the continuous union with Christ, our exalted Lord.*[5] This will become clearer as we consider yet another aspect of this idea.

[5] Cf. R. Schnackenburg, "Nachfolge Christi," *Der Christ und die Weltwirklichkeit* (Wien, 1960) 9-20; A. Schulz, *Nachfolgen und Nachahmen* (Müchen, 1962) 180-186; E. Larsson, *Christus als Vorbild. Eine Untersuchung zu den paulinischen Tauf- und Eikontexten* (Uppsala, 1962), especially informative and enlightening for this aspect; C. M. Proudfoot, "Imitation or Realistic Participation?," *Interpretation* 17 (1963) 140-160.

2 Dying and rising with Christ
in our temporal destiny

The Apostle has made even fuller use of this notion in relation to the Christian's temporal course and condition. His own experience collaborated in this, that is, his apostolic existence during which he was constantly subject to suffering, persecutions, and dangers (1 Cor 4:9-13; 2 Cor 6:4-10, 11:23-33). In a life constantly threatened by death, he saw that he was a follower of Christ, who had preceded him along a way of suffering and death. It is not, however, merely a matter of imitating Christ—merely a re-enactment of Christ's fate—but it is at the same time a profound inner union with him. For this reason Paul develops ideas that have not mistakenly been termed a "mysticism of suffering."[6]

In this connection one of the most significant passages is 2 Corinthians 4:10-18. After the Apostle has glanced back at his painful but unbroken existence, he remarks: "Always bearing about in our body the dying of Jesus so that the life also of Jesus may be made manifest in our bodily frame. For we the living are constantly being handed over to death for Jesus' sake, that the life also of Jesus may be made manifest in our mortal flesh" (v. 10-11). Paul's sufferings are a manifestation of Jesus' death, are the "sufferings of Christ," as he says in the same epistle but in an earlier chapter: "For as the

[6] Cf. J. Schneider, *Die Passionsmystik des Paulus* (Leipzig, 1929); E. W. Wilson, "The Development of Paul's Doctrine of Dying and Rising Again with Christ," *Expository Times* 42 (1931) 562-565; see also references cited above, note 3; for a discussion see Schnackenburg, *Baptism* 178-187.

sufferings of Christ abound in us, so also through Christ does our comfort abound" (1:5). Paul is then convinced that he must sustain the trials and pains of his office as an apostle, not only for the sake of Christ but also in union with his Lord, so that Christ's sufferings might be visible in him. He lived in the conscious awareness of his weakness and his hardships, and that in him Christ crucified vicariously revealed his sufferings to the world.

But the Apostle does not concentrate solely on the thought of suffering and death. For him the cross and Jesus' resurrection forge an inseparable unity. Thus, he knows with the assurance of faith that Jesus' life will some day also manifest itself in his body, namely, as he remarks to the Philippians, that Christ upon his return "will change our lowly body to be like his glorious body" (3:21). He sustains Christ's sufferings for the sake of Christ's future glory. We know by what follows in verse 14 that in the passage from 2 Corinthians Paul is thinking of the glorification of the body at the resurrection: "We know that he who raised up Jesus will raise us also with Jesus." Once again we meet the typically Pauline expression "with Jesus." It is noteworthy that in this context Paul invariably speaks about "Jesus" and not about "Christ." He is reflecting on the once crucified and now risen Jesus, in whose death and resurrection he is incorporated, so that, if he is to share in Jesus' resurrection at the moment of eschatological perfection, he must first in his own temporal existence assume these sufferings with Jesus.

Finally, he indicates his apostolic and missionary convictions when, in a characteristic turn of his thought, he states in verse 12: "Thus death is at work in us, but life in you." Through his own suffering in union with Jesus, Paul wants to be a cause of the Corinthians receiving the fullest possible measure of the strength and glory of their risen Lord. In Colossians he writes even more pointedly: "I rejoice now in the sufferings I bear for your sake; and what is lacking of the sufferings of Christ I fill up in my flesh for his body, which is the church" (1:24).[7]

Even though Paul's "mysticism of suffering" expresses thoughts that are very personal and particularly meaningful to him as an apostle, he is nevertheless convinced that every Christian must resemble his suffering Lord. He expresses this most concisely in a passage from Romans, where he calls us "heirs with Christ": "We suffer with him that we may also be glorified with him," and he adds, "For I reckon that the sufferings of the present time are not worthy to be compared with the glory to come that will be revealed in us" (8:17f.). The course from suffering to glory, determined by God for Jesus to follow, becomes a rule of life for every Christian. It is not only a general law of our human, temporal existence, but it is imposed by reason of our close association with Christ—one with him, we must follow this course with and in imitation of him.

In a frequently quoted text from Galatians, the Apostle resumes his consideration of this notion of our Chris-

[7] Cf. J. Kremer, *Was an den Leiden Christi noch mangelt* (Bonn, 1956); G. Le Grelle, "La plénitude de la parole dans la pauvreté de la chair d'après Col 1, 24," *Nouvelle Revue Théol.* 91 (1959) 232-250.

tian existence: "I have been crucified with Christ; it is
no longer I who live, but Christ who lives in me"
(2:19f.). From what moment is Paul constantly crucified with Christ? If we reflect more closely upon this
passage (which here we cannot do at length,[8] Paul
could only mean that moment in which he became a
Christian. And although he speaks in the first person
singular, he means, nevertheless, every Christian who
from the moment of baptism and through baptism has
been signed by Christ's cross. To express it even more
precisely, the Christian is one who has been drawn
into the event of crucifixion. At the same time the life
of Christ, the risen Lord, becomes operative in the
Christian: no longer is it his own ego, but Christ himself living in him, as Paul remarks in an unparalleled
formulation.

In this passage, and in others as well, we recognize
that the Apostle regards Christ's resurrection as a
power already present in the Christian. He speaks
about this power which he receives as an apostle
from his living Lord, when he declares to the Corinthians that he must take a more forceful stand on the
occasion of his next visit: "Christ is not weak in dealing with you, but is powerful in you. For he was crucified in weakness, but lives by the power of God. And
we are weak in him, but in dealing with you we shall
live with him by the power of God" (2 Cor 13:3f.).
Likewise, it is the risen Christ who consoles and

[8] Cf. H. Schlier, *Der Brief an die Galater*, rev. ed. (Göttingen,
1962) 98-103; Schnackenburg, *Baptism* 62-67; for the formula
"Christ in me" cf. A. Wikenhauser, *Die Christusmystik des
Apostels Paulus*, rev. ed. (Freiburg, 1956) 19-25; M. Bouttier,
En Christ (Paris, 1962) 80-85.

strengthens him in the trials of his apostleship: "We are afflicted in every way, but not crushed; perplexed, but not driven to despair; persecuted, but not forsaken; struck down, but not destroyed" (2 Cor 4, 8f.). As contemporary men we should perhaps like to ask whether the Christian faith is only a religion of suffering. But we would misunderstand Paul if we thought that he valued suffering in itself or that he could visualize himself as a Christian only in suffering. The opposite is the case. For every human life does entail trial, distress, as well as pain, and the Apostle teaches us that suffering with Christ is necessary for this temporal order, so that one day we might rise from the dead and obtain life with him. The keynote dominating Paul's temporal existence is joy. Nowhere is this more explicit than in his epistle to the Philippians, written while he was a prisoner in jail; the expressions "to rejoice" and "joy" occur fourteen times. Among them, "But even if I am made the libation for the sacrifice and service of your faith, I am glad and rejoice with you. And in the same way you should be glad also and rejoice with me" (2:71f.). His constant prayers for the Philippians are filled with joy (1:14), and at the conclusion he admonishes them once more, "Rejoice in the Lord always, again I say, rejoice" (4:4). Union with Christ the Lord brings a profound inner joy. Paul counts all else as worthless in comparison to the knowledge of his Lord, a knowledge that surpasses all things. He strives to know him, to share in his sufferings as well as in the strength of his resurrection, and to be conformed to his death so that he might also rise from the dead (3:10f.).

After examining these texts, one thing should be clear, namely, that a vast program for life lies in the conception of suffering with Christ that we might be glorified with him and dying with Christ that we might rise with him. In this connection we shall now devote our attention to the aspect of eschatological fulfillment when we shall rise with Christ, live with him, and reign with him.

III   OUR FUTURE RISING WITH CHRIST

Even when writing to the Thessalonians, in the oldest of his extant epistles, Paul uses words with added nuances: "Since we believe that Jesus died and rose again, even so, through Jesus, God will bring with him those also who have fallen asleep," (1 Thes 4:4). The expression "with him" occurs in both Judeo-apocalyptic and early Christian tradition.[9] In the book of Daniel we read about the "coming of one who appeared as a Son of Man" (7:13), and we later read about the "people of the holy ones of the most high" (7:27). In both places it is said that power and dominion will be conferred: in the former upon the one who is like the Son of Man, and in the latter upon the people (7:27). It is still uncertain in Daniel what relationship exists between the "Son of Man" and the "holy ones of the most high," whether both signify the same thing or whether "the Son of Man" is at the same time an individual and collective form, a representative of all the People of God. In the book of Enoch it is somewhat clearer: "The just and chosen ones will be saved one day and will then no

[9] Cf. J. Dupont, Σὺν Χριστῷ L'union avec le Christ suivant s.Paul, vol. 1 (Bruges, 1952) 80-100.

longer behold the countenance of the sinner and the unjust. The Lord of spirits will then dwell above them, and they will eat *with the Son of Man*" (Ethiopian En 62:13f.). The eschatology of the early Church had already applied the "Son of Man" to Jesus and understood the "chosen ones" to be those trustworthy Christians who would reign with him. Thus, the Apocalypse (20:3) tells us that the martyrs would come to life to rule for a thousand years with Christ (μετὰ τοῦ Χριστοῦ), remarking further (20:6) that they will be priests of God and Christ who will rule for a thousand years with him. The entire early Church, however, was familiar with this idea of an eschatological reign with Christ, and it appears to have belonged to her catechesis (Mt 19:28, 25:34; Lk 22:29f.; 1 Cor 4:8, 6:2; 2 Tim 2:12; Ap 3:21). Paul simply expresses a common doctrine of the early Church, but at the same time permeates it with his own notion of dying and rising with Christ.

The meaning of the words "God will bring us with Jesus" is clear even in the Jewish and early Christian background. At the end of this temporal order God will permit Christ, the Son of Man (Paul, however, avoids this expression, which is misleading for his Hellenistic readers), to appear before the whole world in power and glory, and with him those who belong to Christ, in order that they might live and rule forever with him. Further in the course of his instruction Paul, again employing older apocalyptic language, says to the Thessalonians "For the Lord himself will descend from heaven . . . then we who are alive, who are left, shall be caught up together with them [i.e., those who have been raised from the dead] in the clouds to meet the Lord in the air, and so we shall always be *with the Lord*" (4:16f.). We should not take exception to a mode of expression that employs old images and is bound up with an earlier cosmology. What is decisive is that we will then be united with the Lord forever. At that moment the purpose of all our presently imperceptible fellowship with Christ on earth will be reached, for if we have followed him in suffering and death, have been one with him and conformed to him, we will also share in his heavenly glory and be one with him forever. That this consummation of the final days will be allotted to us in virtue of Jesus' role as Savior and in virtue of our union with him, is clearly indicated by the Apostle: "Since we believe that Jesus died and rose again, even so [οὕτως] through Jesus, God will bring those also who have fallen asleep" (4:14).

We have seen earlier that Paul's hope and longing in his suffering are always directed toward the future resurrection. The fact that he has such strong faith in our suffering now with Christ so that we might one day be "glorified" with him (Rom 8:17), deserves closer scrutiny of his great chapter on the resurrection (1 Cor 15). Here Paul once again leans upon the parallel of Adam and Christ: "For as in Adam all die, so also in Christ shall all be made alive" (v. 22). Toward the end he states even more clearly: "Just as we have borne the image of the man of dust, we shall also bear the image of the man of heaven" (v. 49). The risen Christ, the representative and leader of redeemed mankind, exhibits in his glorified form the example for all men who belong to him and who have been called to the fullness of salvation, and he himself leads them to this fullness of salvation. Christ, the Second Adam, has become "a life-giving spirit" (v. 45); as the raised, living, and exalted Lord he pours out his spirit, the divine "Spirit" of life, upon all who believe and are united with him. In baptism we receive this divine Spirit who dwells and operates in us, until the day when he will also effect the resurrection of our bodies.

In Romans Paul remarks, "If the Spirit of him who raised Jesus from the dead dwells in you, then he who raised Jesus Christ from the dead will give life to your mortal bodies also through his Spirit who dwells in you" (8:11). At the same time it is clear that our future resurrection is a profound mystery of faith, and that we may in no way represent it according to temporal conditions and analogies. It will be a new creation from the divine Spirit of life, who has already been given us, Paul says, as "first fruits" or as a "pledge," a guarantee (Rom 8:23; 2 Cor 1:22, 5:5). Because Jesus as the glorified Christ possesses the fullness of the Spirit and permits him to descend upon us, he is also called the "firstborn among many brethren" (Rom 8:29) or "the firstborn from the dead" (Col 1:18). Our hope depends entirely on Christ, who has been crucified and buried, but who has been raised from the dead by the power of his Father.[10] An old article of faith, taken up

[10] Cf. J. Schmitt, *Jésus ressuscité dans la prédication apostolique* (Paris, 1949) 216-240; Floyd V. Filson, *Jesus Christ the Risen Lord* (New York, 1956); F. X. Durrwell, *The Resurrection, A Biblical Study* (New York, 1960); S. Lyonnet, "La valeur sotériologique de la résurrection du Christ selon s. Paul," *Gregorianum* 39 (1958) 295-318; D. M. Stanley, *Christ's Resurrection in Pauline Soteriology* (Rome, 1961); N. Crotty, "The Redemptive Role of Christ's Resurrection," *Thomist* 25 (1962) 54-106.

by Paul, maintains that Christ was "put to death for our trespasses and raised for our justification" (Rom 4:25). It is in him and through him that we have the guarantee of our own resurrection, and thus we, too, will be raised from the dead and glorified "with him."

CHAPTER VII

Revelation and Faith in the Gospel of John

Faith is the adequate answer to revelation. But what is faith? Is it the conviction and assertion that every-thing God has revealed through the prophets and finally through his Son, all that is written in Holy Scripture is true? Surely, this assent to the truth of revelation is of essential moment in faith. But is that everything? For a long time we have overemphasized this intellectual character of faith and neglected the other aspect, that faith is also personal trust in and obedience to the revealing God. It is discipleship and fellowship with Jesus Christ, the latest messenger of God and bearer of eschatological revelation and salva-tion. The biblical concept of faith is directed more to these personal categories of thought, and it reflects more the existential attitude and conduct of man before God. There is an encounter between the revealing God and the believing man: a call and challenge on the part of God; a response and decision on the part of man. This is especially true of the revelation-event that took place in Jesus Christ.

If one reads through the New Testament observing in particular the references made to faith, it becomes clear that John's gospel reveals a mature concept of faith. In the synoptics, faith is strongly bound to the situation (for example, belief in the miracles of healing), or it is understood as a charismatic power (Mk 11:22). But in John faith is the basic decision and attitude of man when he is faced with the eschatological revelation of Jesus, which brings him salvation. For John faith is situated in the narrative of the earthly works of Jesus. These are the words of Jesus, which always have for him a deeper meaning, as well as the works of Jesus, which he considers "signs" and which offer a decisive moment both to the believer in his historical situation and to the believing reader. We are dealing here with a rather complex dialectic between revelation and faith. For the Evangelist faith is not simply believing in Jesus because of his wondrous works and his magnificent words; nor does revelation simply open the door to faith. That we might better understand revelation and faith in John's gospel let us first make a short comparison between Mark's account and that of John.

I   REVELATION AND FAITH IN MARK AND JOHN

In Mark's gospel concerning the earthly works of Jesus we find a record of his words and acts, which corresponds very closely to the imaginative picture we have of Christ. We hear of Jesus' preaching and doctrine, his acts of authority and self-manifestations, until the passion puts an end to these works and the message of the resurrection places these obscure events in a new light. But Jesus, as Mark portrays him, acts curiously, incomprehensibly, and even contradictorily. He seeks to gain many followers, and people do flock to him in order to learn; he heals many who are sick. But then on occasion he withdraws from the crowds, seeks solitude, and instructs his disciples apart from the people. He causes a sensation by his "teaching with authority" and by casting out devils; but when these evil spirits, who recognize him as the "Son of God," blasphemously cry out, he forbids them to reveal his identity. Likewise, those whom he heals are asked to keep silent. The people do not understand him. Even his disciples do not understand his words and doctrine. He explains much to them personally, but when three of them see Jesus transfigured on the mountain, he forbids them to speak of it until "the Son of Man has risen from the dead" (Mk 9:8). Jesus flees from the crowds, and yet we see him among the people teaching and healing, sending out the Twelve to preach and to cast out devils. This is indeed a curious representation. Christ seemingly wants to reveal himself but, nevertheless, does everything to keep himself hidden. We are almost tempted to say with the brethren in John's gospel: "No man works in secret if he seeks to be known openly. If you do these things, show yourself to the world" (Jn 7:4). Even here we can detect a parallel, in spite of all the differences in the two evangelists. These apparent contradictions in Mark's treatment of the behavior of Jesus has led us to speak of the "Messiah-mystery" in his gospel. There is much discussion among the exegetes in trying to understand the meaning of Mark's portrayal of Jesus.[1] We cannot go into this problem now, but we might say briefly that this so-called Messiah-mystery must be viewed in the context of the Evangelist's theological intention, which looks back upon the entire life of Jesus from the post-resurrection standpoint of the Christian community.

If here one goes from Mark's to John's representation of Jesus, Christ's revelation of himself appears more complex. If in Mark Jesus had taken pains to preserve his secret, then in the fourth gospel he reveals himself without qualification to individual men, for example, to the Samaritan woman (Jn 4:26), the man born blind whom he healed (9:37), Martha (11:25f.), his disciples (14:9f.), and even publicly to skeptic Jews (5:19-30, 6:32-58, 7:37f., 8:12, etc.). He does not order anyone

[1] Selected bibliography to the "Messiah-mystery" in the gospel of Mark: W. Wrede, *Das Messiasgeheimnis in den Evangelien* (Göttingen, 1901, 3rd ed., 1963); E. Bickermann, "Das Messiasgeheimnis und die Komposition des Markusevangeliums," *ZNW* 22 (1923) 122-140; H. J. Ebeling, *Das Messiasgeheimnis und die Botschaft des Markus-Evangelisten* (Berlin, 1939); E. Sjöberg, *Der verborgene Menschensohn in den Evangelien* (Lund, 1955); T. A. Burkill, "The Injunctions to Silence in St. Mark's Gospel," *Theologische Zeitschrift* 12 (1956) 585-604; "Strain in the Secret; An Examination of Mark 11, 1=13,37," *ZNW* 51 (1960) 31-46; "The Hidden Son of Man in St. Mark's Gospel." *ZNW* 52 (1961) 189=213; G. H. Boobyer, "The Secrecy Motif in St. Mark's Gospel," *New Testament Studies* 6 (1959, 1960) 225-235; G. Strecker, "Zur Messiasgeheimnis-Theorie im Markusvangelium," *Studia Evangelica*, vol. 3 (Berlin, 1964) 87-104; E. Schweizer, "Zur Frage des Messiasgeheimnisses bei Markus," *ZNW* 56 (1965) 1-8; U. Luz, "Das Geheimnismotiv und die markinische Christologie," *ZNW* 56 (1965) 9-30.

to be silent, and he appears filled with urgency to bear witness to himself as "the Son," "the Light of the World," "the Bread from Heaven," the "Good Shepherd," and so on. Upon entering Jerusalem he immediately stands before the Jews and says God is his Father and makes himself equal to God (5:17f.). Without qualification he advances his self-revelation still further: "For as the Father raises the dead and gives them life, even so the Son also gives life to whom he will. The Father judges no one, but all judgment he has given to the Son, that all may honor the Son even as they honor the Father" (5:21ff.). The ἐγώ εἰμί expressions in John imitate the Old Testament theophany formulas; therefore, Jesus applies the Old Testament self-manifestation of God himself. "We must work the works of him who sent me while it is day; night comes, when no one can work. As long as I am in the world, I am the light of the world" (9:4f.). This is the predominant tone throughout the discourses of Jesus' public mission.

If one compares the conduct of Jesus as found in Mark with that found in John, there is complete contradiction. We recognized that Mark pursues a theological purpose in drawing his picture of Jesus, even though it is historically probable that Jesus did wish to preserve his secret. In John, however, there is a tendency toward the opposite direction: Jesus must sufficiently reveal himself through his discourses and works, which are "signs," so that he might bear witness to what he is. The thought of the Evangelist is perhaps most powerfully expressed in the words of Jesus to his disciples, "If I had not come and spoken to them, they would not have sin; but now they have no excuse for their sin. . . . If I had not done among them the works which no one else did, they would not have sin; but now they have seen and hated both me and my Father" (Jn 15:22, 24). The unbelievers cannot be excused; the revelation of Jesus, as the eschatological messenger sent from God, was clear and sufficiently convincing for all to have believed. However, the Jews refused to believe, just as their forefathers had done, and hence fell into the dark, hateful, and deadly enmity which gave birth to unbelief. This is what deeply motivates the Evangelist. He takes pains to open to his readers the shining clarity and ultimate depth of Christ's revelation. He desires, as he himself states, to strengthen them in their faith, that "Jesus is the Christ, the Son of God, and that believing you may have life in his name" (20:31).

II REVELATION AND ITS RELATION TO FAITH ACCORDING TO JOHN

If one carefully reads John and pays particular attention to remarks that could be significant for the historical situation, one discovers that Jesus could not have spoken more openly and definitely. There are three examples. First, the word of the brethren to him, "No man works in secret if he seeks to be known openly. If you do these things, show yourself to the world" (Jn 7:4). In the opinion of these skeptical, unbelieving relatives Jesus had not sufficiently manifested himself to the "world" in Judea and Jerusalem. Again, the Jews at the feast of the dedication surround

him and ask, "How long will you keep us in suspense?
If you are the Christ, tell us plainly (10:24). Jesus answers: "I told you, and you do not believe. The works
that I do in my Father's name, they bear witness to me;
but you do not believe because you do not belong to
my sheep" (10:25). One may not directly apply his
answer "I told you" to the Messiah-question; but if we
investigate, we see that nowhere in John's account does
Jesus actually call himself the Messiah.[2] We are inclined to attribute this title to him because he desig-
nates himself constantly as "the Son" and this in our
opinion implies a messianic title. This is a critical point.
John knows that Jesus, seen historically, has never
publicly claimed himself to be the Messiah, that is, the
Messiah in the Jewish sense. But he is convinced that
Jesus through his life, his discourses, and his works
has clearly revealed his identity as the bearer of salvation in a much higher sense, namely, as the only Son
of God, the Christ in the sense professed by the Christian community. In the great theological discourses of
Christ the Evangelist makes explicit this unique title of
Jesus, which was only implicit in the behavior of the
historical Jesus, that is, in his words and deeds. It would
be seen by those who wished to see and believe. The
Johannine Jesus indicates this in his answer to the Jews,
"The works that I do in the name of my Father, these
bear witness to me" (v. 25).

Insofar as the great discourses and miracles of Jesus
openly declare and reveal his claim to be the eschato-

[2] Cf. R. Schnackenburg, "Die Messiasfrage im Johannesevangelium," *Neutestamentliche Aufsätze*, Festschrift für Prof J.
Schmid (Regensburg, 1963) 240-264.

logical prophet and bearer of salvation, "the Son" and "Son of Man," who has come down from heaven, they explicate faith. This becomes especially evident in John's notion of "miracle." In John's gospel miracles are called "signs" and are for the reader ostensible works of Jesus, for example, the healing of a man who was sick for thirty-eight years (5), the multiplication of loaves (6), the cure of the man born blind (9), the resurrection of Lazarus, dead four days and in process of decay (11). But still "the Jews did not believe." Who then comprehended these "signs" for what they were? Only the believing disciples, of whom as early as the first "sign"—the changing of water into wine—it was emphatically said: "And his disciples believed in him" (2:11).

If we recall that Mark frequently described the disciples as slow to understand, imprudent, even hard-hearted, then we will point out our third example in John's gospel which is seldom observed. In spite of the faith the disciples seem to have, they often misconstrue or at times fail to understand at all the words of Jesus even in the Upper Room. This is frequently an artistic device used in the fourth gospel to clarify the revelation discourses and obviate such "misunderstandings." But there is also a passage that cannot be so easily explained. In his final address to his disciples Jesus says, "I have said this to you in figures. The hour is coming, when I shall no longer speak to you in figures but tell you plainly of the Father" (Jn 16:25). The disciples again misunderstand Jesus: they say, "Ah, now you are speaking plainly, not in any figure" (16:29). Jesus actually means that his previous discourse to them was not yet "plainly" obvious to them. It would seem then that his words, which to the reader sound so undisguised, appear in a different light; the Johannine Jesus himself treats them here as "figures," as words with a hidden meaning that cannot be understood at this moment. After Easter, or as can be anticipated in the sense of the Evangelist—through the promised Spirit—they will first yield their fully developed revelation.

Therefore, John's gospel testifies that the earthly revelation of Jesus, seen historically, was not as public as the reader might think. It was thus construed by the believing insight of the Evangelist that each person who was ready to believe could come to faith. This is the problem of revelation and faith. One scholar rightly said, "In John's gospel all is evident, all is expressed, but the veil lies in the unbelief of the 'world'. They demand signs (6:30), which are already there; they ask to be told openly (10:24) what has already been spoken to them. They wish to force Jesus to reveal himself (7:4) and he has already done so." He says further that in another way, no less effective than in Mark's gospel, the Messiah-mystery is also present and operative in John's gospel: "We see that John understands the Messiah-mystery much more radically: glory (*doxa*) need not hide itself (through commands of silence), as it is hidden in the other gospels. Rather the revealing or concealing function of Jesus' self-revelation is reflected in man's belief and unbelief."[3]

Thus in John's gospel it becomes especially clear what revelation and faith are according to the New Testa-

[3] H. Schulte, *Der Begriff der Offenbarung im Neuen Testament* (München, 1949) 19.

ment.[4] Revelation cannot be fully grasped in a rational manner, but it requires an answer coming from the totality of human behavior and from personal decision. First there must be an act of total submission, inner assent, and personal commitment (6:68), which, of course, includes the conviction that Jesus is "the Holy One of God" (6:69). Then it becomes a task for the believer to penetrate his faith with a progressive understanding, just as Jesus' words indicate: "If I am not doing the works of my Father, then do not believe me; but if I do them, even though you do not believe me, believe the works, that you may know and understand that the Father is in me and I am in the Father" (10:37f.). That is the progress *a fide ad intellectum*. Rational knowledge is not completely excluded; we must question the foundations of our faith, and then our faith will not be irrational. Yet in the final analysis we can "prove" nothing, especially to the unbeliever.

Likewise rational knowledge is neither an adequate nor sufficient attitude toward faith, because the revelation accepted in faith calls man to action. Jesus says, "If any man's will is to do his will [that is, the one who sent him], he shall know whether the teaching is from God or whether I am speaking on my own authority" (7:17). Revelation challenges the entire man with all

[4] For the notion of revelation in the New Testament see also H. H. Huber, *Der Begriff der Offenbarung im Johannesevangelium* (Göttengen, 1934); E. F. Scott, *The New Testament Idea of Revelation* (New York, 1935); W. Bulst, *Offenbarung. Biblischer und theologischer Begriff* (Düsseldorf, 1960), and American ed. *Revelation* (New York, 1965); R. Schnackenburg, "Zum Offenbarungsgedanken in der Bibel," *BZ* 7 (1963) 2-22; H.-D. McDonald, *Theories of Revelation (1860-1960)* (London, 1963); R. Latourelle, *Théologie de la Révélation* (Bruges, 1963).

his powers; it touches the very core of his personal being and leads him to a crisis, to the situation of a personal decision. In the very depths of his being as a person, man must decide before the challenge of God's revelation, whether he believes in his salvation or desires to shut himself off in unbelief, committing himself to destruction and destroying the last possible way of salvation offered to him. "He who believes in him is not condemned; he who does not believe is condemned already, because he has not believed in the name of the only Son of God" (3:18). In the eschatological revelation of the Son salvation becomes effective, and therefore faith signifies the realization of salvation for the individual man, the personal acceptance of God's offer of salvation brought by his Son. But unbelief signifies the self-exclusion of salvation; "the wrath of God rests upon him" (3:36).

Thus faith corresponding to divine revelation and exercising its function of salvation obtains a unique significance with regard to the historical and eschatological mission of Jesus. This last Revealer and Mediator of our salvation has but once stepped forth into human history: "No one has ascended into heaven but he who descended from heaven 'the Son of Man'" (3:13). In another passage the Johannine Jesus declares, "No one comes to the Father but by me . . . who has seen me, has seen the Father" (14:6, 9). It is clear that here to "see" means to believe, the proper way of participating in the salvific mission of the Son and of entering community with the Father. But in order to grasp the very nature of faith according to John, we will further examine his manner of reflecting upon belief in Jesus the Christ, the Son of God.

III   THE NATURE OF FAITH ACCORDING TO JOHN

One can arrive at an understanding of what faith is for John from an analysis of his mode of speaking, the linguistic structures he uses, and the various expressions he employs to convey his theology of faith.[5] John's idea of faith is not an abstract notion. The substantive "faith" ($\pi\iota\sigma\tau\iota\varsigma$) does not appear outside of 1 John 5:4. Instead, we find the verb "to believe," mostly with "in" ($\pi\iota\sigma\tau\epsilon\upsilon\epsilon\iota\nu$ $\epsilon\iota\varsigma$ thirty-six times in the gospel). How is this used and what does it mean? Does it mean an acknowledgment of Jesus? Does it mean a trusting union with him? Whatever it means, it implies in every case an intimate relation of the believer with Jesus. The

[5] Selected bibliography for faith in John's gospel: J. Huby, "La connaissance de foi dans s. Jean," *Recherches de Science Relig.* 21 (1931) 385-421; F.-M. Braun, "L'accueil de foi selon s. Jean," *Vie Spirituelle* 92 (1955) 344-363; M. Bonningues, *La foi dans l'Evangile de s. Jean* (Paris, 1955); D. Mollat, "La foi dans le quatrième évangile," *Lumière et Vie* 22 (1955) 515-531; G. L. Phillips, "Faith and Vision in the Fourth Gospel," *Studies in the Fourth Gospel*, ed. F. L. Cross (London, 1957) 83-96; A. Decourtray, "La conception johannique de la foi," *NRT* 91 (1959) 561-576; R. Bultman, "$\pi\iota\sigma\tau\epsilon\upsilon\omega$ bei Johannes," *ThWNT* 6 (1959) 224-230; W. Grundmann, "Verständnis und Bewegung des Glaubens im Johannesevangelium," *Kerygma und Dogma* 6 (1960) 131-154; H. Schlier, "Glauben, Erkennen und Lieben nach dem Johannesevangelium," *Besinnung auf das Neue Testament* (Freiburg, 1964) 279-293; F.-M. Willcox, *La notion de foi dans le quatrième évangile* (dissertation, Louvain, 1962); R. Schnackenburg, *Das Johannesevangelium*, vol. 1 (Freiburg, 1965) 508-524.

object of faith is always the person of Jesus (14:1 is only an apparent exception), and this is by no means accidental. Since Jesus reveals himself as the only Son of God throughout the fourth gospel, faith becomes the assent to this self-revelation. But because he declares that whoever believes in him possesses eternal life (3:16, 18, 36, 6:29, 40, etc.), and this life is present in him (5:26, 6:57, 11:25, 14:6), faith also unites the believer with Christ the Mediator of eternal life.

Faith is recognition of Jesus' claim to be the one sent by God (6:29, 11:42, 16:27, 30, 17:8, 21), the only begotten Son (3:18), the Son of Man (9:35), the Messiah, the Son of God (11:27, 20:31). Other figurative self-pronouncements of Jesus (ἐγώ εἰμί) underscore the importance of his coming and are meant as an object of belief: he is the "Bread from Heaven" (6:32-35, 49-51), the "Light of the World" (8:12, 9:5, 12:35f.), the "Door" (10:7, 9), the "Good Shepherd" (10:11, 14), the "Resurrection and the Life" (11:25), the "Way and the Truth, and the Life" (14:6), or the mere "I am" (8:24, 28, 58, 13:19).[6] But this faith in the person of Christ is also personal fellowship with him (8:12) and discipleship (8:31). It is a complete self-surrender to Christ, who alone leads men from death to life, from the world below to the celestial world of God (5:24, 10:9f., 12:32, 14:6). All this is expressed by the for-

[6] Cf. E. Schweizer, *Ego eimi* . . . (Göttingen, 1939); J. Richter, *Ani Hu und Ego eimi* (dissertation, Erlangen, 1956); H. Zimmermann, "Das absolute Ἐγώ εἰμί als die neutestamentliche Offenbarungsformel," *BZ* 4 (1960) 54-59, 266-276; "Das absolute Ich bin in der Redeweise Jesu," *Trierer Theol. Zeitschrift* 69 (1960) 1-20; S. Schultz, *Komposition und Herkunft der Johanneischen Reden* (Stuttgart, 1960) 70-131.

mula "to believe in him." It does not exclusively mean trust or assent but rather both, and more: it means a complete personal commitment to Christ, the sole bearer of revelation and salvation. We can understand the absolute use of the verb "to believe" (thirty times) only through the context in which it appears. But here we generally notice the same meaning as explored above; the short expression signifies Johannine faith in its full sense—to believe in Christ as the light and life of man, the Messiah, and Son of God (1:7, 50, 4:41, 42, 53, 6:36, 47, 64, etc.).

More attention must be paid to the use of "believe" with the dative (eighteen times). It is frequently emphasized that this usage has no essentially different meaning than "to believe in." But closer scrutiny proves that persons and objects other than Jesus appear in the dative: the Father who has sent Jesus (5:24), Scripture (2:22), Moses (5:46) and his writings (5:47), as well as the works of Jesus (10:38). We can discover the meaning of this usage from John 5:31-47: the dative signifies the *witness* or *witnesses*, everyone and everything that testifies to Jesus. Here in the series of witnesses John the Baptist, the only human witness, stands first (v. 33-35), then the works given to Jesus by his Father (v. 36), the Father himself (v. 37), Scripture (v. 39ff.), and finally Moses and his writing (v. 46f.). Jesus himself also testifies to his revelation, and his own testimony is true because he knows whence he has come and whither he is going (8:14). But there is another witness who testifies to him: the Father who has sent him (8:17). There is a unity of his own testimony with that of the Father. Therefore, to believe his simple words is the highest motive of faith (10:37, 14:11, cf. 4:48, 50).

Theologically, it is most important that faith rely upon witness and witnesses. It is possible for all men of good will, for all seeking faith, to assent to the message of Christ. John's proof is not a matter of pure reason, but of witness, a distinctive form of revelation. It enlightens man's reason, but does not dispense him from the responsibility of making his own decision, and of submitting himself in obedient faith (3:36) to the revelation of God in Jesus Christ. This is generally true of faith in the New Testament but is made explicit only by John, who emphasizes that the testimony of the earthly witnesses continues in the Church through the intercession of the Holy Spirit (Jn 15:26, 16:13f.; 1 Jn 1:1-3, 5:6ff.). Other related expressions from the same linguistic ambit make the personal union of the believer with the Revealer still more clear. In John's prologue we find the phrase "they did not receive him" (1:11), and this compound verb ($\pi\alpha\rho\alpha\lambda\alpha\mu\beta\acute{\alpha}\nu\epsilon\iota\nu$) is taken up in the next verse by the simple verb ($\lambda\alpha\mu\beta\acute{\alpha}\nu\epsilon\iota\nu$), which we must literally translate "all who accepted him." We find this mode of expression in a similar sense again in 5:43 and 13:20. The same meaning is found in the expressions "to accept our witness" (3:11) and "to accept my words" (12:48, 17:8). He who receives the words of Jesus and interiorly assimilates them (17:8), assimilates with the revelation of the Revealer himself, and recognizes that Jesus is the one sent by God (3:53f.).

The image of Jesus' "coming" to men corresponds to the image of believers coming to Jesus (in John 6:35 this expresses the same as believing in him, a mode of

expression that continues in verses 37, 44ff., and 65).
One recognizes in it the image of the flock: the Father
entrusts to the Son all who will belong to the flock and
leads them to the Son. The Son does not drive away
those who come to him (6:38, cf. 17:12), but rather embraces them lest they go astray. Although John considers the believer's relationship with Jesus a personal
one, he is mindful of the fact that the believers form a
community intended by the Father. Wherever the
moral character of the decision in faith is stressed, the
Evangelist speaks of a "coming" to Jesus, as under the
symbol of light in 3:20f. ("to come to the light"), and
negatively in 5:40. Jesus can invite men to come to him
in faith: "If any one thirst, let him come to me and
drink" (7:37). To the same perspective belongs the
"following" of Jesus (1:37f., 41, 44), which in 8:12 is
a following in faith, and in 10:4, 5, 27 a following in the
flock of Jesus, the true shepherd.

To believe also means *to hear* the voice or words of
Jesus (5:24, 6:45, 8:43, 47, etc.), to hear in the sense
of obeying (3:36). Here the correspondence between
faith and revelation is also shown. To hear must be
an interior listening, a learning from the Father (6:45),
an acceptance of and commitment to the word of the
Revealer. The faithful must "abide" in the word of
Jesus (8:31).

Other verbs within the ambit of "to believe" are "to
see" (6:40, 12:45), and "to know."[7] To see Jesus in
faith is to perceive his glory and to believe in the in-

[7] Cf. R. Bultmann, "γινώσκω," ThWNT 1 (1933) 712f., and also
πιστεύω," 6 (1959) 228ff.; F.-M. Willcox, *La notion de foi* 152-
173; H. Schlier (see above, note 5); J. Gaffney, S. J., "Believing
and Knowing in the Fourth Gospel," *Theological Studies* 26
(1965) 215-241.

carnation of the Word (1:14, cf. 1:51). By him and in him one sees the Father (14:9). Terms expressing "to know" are especially numerous, and the proximity of knowing and believing is often noticed and underscored. The Johannine "to know" is many-sided. In relation to faith it sometimes means an advanced understanding (6:69, 10:38, 14:20), not simply in the sense of a greater rational understanding, but rather as "an understanding which is proper to faith."[8] One must always remember that "to know" in the biblical sense is an act creating a community or deepening the community. Thereby, faith can certainly develop into knowledge, and knowledge is an element of faith, but faith is always presupposed and obtains greater clarity and depth only through knowledge (6:69). Abiding in Christ, the believer continues to grow in knowledge and love (17:26). The two ideas are correlative: faith opens man for a deeper understanding of and an intimate union with Christ, but this knowledge is connected with faith, and therefore is different from Gnostic or mystical knowledge.

The Johannine faith is also intimately connected with the idea "to confess." Although we seldom find this infinitive expression (ὁμολογεῖν), we do hear of confessions of faith. The Evangelist reports the confessions of individuals (Nathanael, 1:49; Simon-Peter, 6:18; the blind man, 9:38; Martha, 11:27; Thomas, 20:25) and of groups (the Samaritans, 4:42; the Galileans, 6:14). These confessions of faith, directed against the unbelief and disbelief of the Evangelist's contemporaries, are Christological.

[8] An expression of R. Bultmann, *ThWNT* 1 (1933) 713, line 21.

Finally, faith stands in a closer relation to discipleship. The faith of the "Twelve" is often highlighted when the Evangelist wishes to underscore trials and triumph (2:11, 6:6, 67ff., 13:19, 14:1-14). The resurrection of Jesus is a further step for the believing disciples (20:8, 25-29). Faith is a resolute following of Jesus, steadfastness with him, abiding in his word (8:31).

The character of Johannine faith is more clearly represented in the relationship of the linguistic ambit of "to believe" with other significant ideas: acceptance of the proclaimed revelation through Jesus, acceptance of the Revealer and Mediator himself, personal fellowship with him in a growing understanding, open confession, and active love according to his precepts and his example.

The deepest mystery, however, is that faith is *grace*.[9] The Evangelist comes to this conclusion through his reflection on the dark enigma of unbelief. It can appear contradictory that in the fourth gospel Jesus gives the proof of faith (10:37f.), invites people to believe (12:35f.), and at the same time considers the faithful as a group entrusted to him by the Father, as men who hear his voice (6:37ff., 8:47, 10:27, 18:37). But these different aspects depend upon the context and theological perspective of the Evangelist.

The prime text denoting faith as grace is found in the discourse about the Bread from Heaven (Jn 6). After his self-revelation (v. 32-35) Jesus firmly states, "But I said to you that you have seen me and yet do not believe" (v. 36). He goes on to say that he rejects no one

[9] Cf. A. Vanhoye, "Notre foi oeuvre divine, d'après le quatrième évangile," *Nouvelle Revue Théol.* 96 (1964) 337-354.

whom the Father leads to him (v. 37-40). Jesus wishes
to explain the hard reality of unbelief. After the mur-
murings of the Jews (v. 41f.) he begins anew and speaks
about the work of the Father, "No one can come to me
unless the Father who sent me draws him" (v. 44). The
final quotation and its application is difficult to interpret (v. 45).[10] Undoubtedly it means that the Father
initially draws men to Jesus and thus absolutely stands
at the beginning. At the end of the discourse Jesus with
the same reality firmly states, "But there are some of
you that do not believe" (v. 64), and he says further,
"This is why I told you that no one can come to me
unless it is granted him by the Father" (v. 65).

Reproving the unbelief of the Jews Jesus objects that
they cannot bear to hear his word (8:43). They are of
their father, the devil, and their will is to do their
father's desires (v. 44). Why do they not believe in
him? "Because you are not of God" (v. 47).

In John 10 we find the image of the faithful flock entrusted to Jesus. The fellowship of the sheep with their
shepherd (v. 3f.) and their deep mutual "knowing"
(v. 14f.) are expressed in the figurative discourse. The
Father is the authentic Master of the flock and has entrusted the sheep to his Son, the Good Shepherd. Jesus
receives this charge from his Father (v. 17f.), and those
who believe belong to his flock (v. 25). They who do
not believe do not belong to his sheep, and therefore
do not hear his voice (v. 26ff.). The sheep are given to

[10] Besides the commentaries, cf. P. Borgen, *Bread from Heaven*
(Leiden, Netherlands, 1965) 83ff; E. D. Freed, *Old Testament
Quotations in the Gospel of John* (Leiden, 1965) 17-20.

Jesus by the Father, and no one is able to snatch them from the Father's hand (v. 29).

This idea of faith is also brought out in the high priestly prayer (Jn 17). Jesus speaks of his disciples who believe in him and faithfully persevere with him, "Thine they were, and thou gavest them to me" (v. 6). Certain men whom the Father has given to the Son constitute the flock of the believers. Such men are also thought of as the children of God scattered throughout the world, whom Jesus should gather into one through his death (11:52). Therefore, in the first epistle of John, the Christian community understands itself as a community of the children of God, separated from all who are "of the world" (1 Jn 2:19ff.; 4:4ff.).

There is another aspect in Jesus' discourses, one that explains unbelief by *moral guilt*. The proneness to evil hinders men from coming to the light (Jn 3:19ff.). They seek their own honor and not the glory of God (5:44). They prove themselves through their covetousness to be children of the devil (8:44), and their blindness becomes delusion (9:39f.). In the eyes of the Evangelist their stubbornness is self-incriminating (9:40; 12:42f.). There is no justification for unbelief, since Jesus is revealed by his words and works (15:22ff.). Unbelief in this sense is the absolute sin (16:9). The Evangelist does not equate the moral guilt of men with divine predestination. This is not contradictory, as faith is based simultaneously upon a free decision of man and the grace of God. He conceives faith as a decision, because it is the answer to revelation, the assent to the call issued through the Revealer. Through reflection on unbelief the Evangelist comes upon the insight that God himself must draw man and lead him to Jesus.

This sums up the essence of the eschatological revelation in Jesus Christ: it is the proclamation of God which is intended to lead all men to salvation, but which each man must heed and answer in faith; it is the last decisive offer of God, which places man in a decision-situation; it is a self-witness of God in his Son, which man must seal with his faith (3:33).

CHAPTER VIII

Community with God
According to John

A fundamental and predominant notion of Johannine theology is that of community with God, found in a living union with Christ through faith. For several reasons this theme is of special interest.

First, we recognize how vividly John (the great theologian behind the fourth gospel and the first epistle of John)[1] has taken up human religious feeling and longing and has responded with the fundamentals of Christian belief. For the thought of community with God is to be found in some form or other in every religion, inasmuch as the yearning for nearness to God along with awe-inspiring fear of him belong to man's fundamental religious sentiments. John, however, has given

---

[1] For our purpose we can pass over the question of who this great theologian was and whether the author of the fourth Gospel and of the first epistle of John is identical. In any case, it is the same school of religious thought. Cf. R. Schnackenburg, *Die Johannesbriefe*, rev. ed. (Freiburg, 1963) 34-38. This chapter is a revised excursus from that commentary (p. 66-72).

this notion an unmistakable form that leads us to the very center of the Christian faith.

Second, it enables us to compare Johannine thought with other ideas and religious currents then prevalent and to grasp the distinctive character of Christian faith and hope in its environment. This religio-historical comparison is important in order to see the correlation with contemporaneous modes of expression as well as the originality and essence of Christianity. It is greatly disputed as to where the main roots and influences of Johannine theology lie. Too frequently one does not duly consider both the creative power and the adaptability of the early Church, which integrated current terms and concepts while still preserving her own tradition and viewpoint. The lesson we can learn from such probing is how to accommodate ourselves to our own times without sacrificing the substance of our faith; how to express and transmit the Christian message to modern men.

Seen from this point of view, our theme is most meaningful. In modern times the very notion of God has become problematic and disputable for many people, even Christians. Can we think of and refer to God as we have in the past? Should we imagine that he dwells in heaven and rules over the universe? That he lives in a transcendent world separated from our empirical one? Should we not see God as immanent within our world, as indwelling in the "depth of our human existence"?[2]

[2] Cf. the book of Bishop John A. T. Robinson, *Honest to God* (London, 1963), which has caused so great a discussion; cf. *Diskussion zu Bischof Robinsons Gott ist anders*, ed. H. W. Augustin (München, 1964).

John teaches us that this notion of God and of our relation to him was present in Christianity from its very beginning, and that it was effective for the Christian life, even though the ancient view of the world was not abandoned. In Johannine theology we get an approach to God not alien to our mind: God is spirit (Jn 4:24) and light (1 Jn 1:5) and love (1 Jn 4:8, 16). He is accessible to us in our present earthly life and willing to communicate with us, so that we may participate in his eternal life. But the way to enjoy community with him is presented to us in the salvific mission and message of his Son Jesus Christ.

Community with God is the leading idea in John's first epistle as well as the final point of view in his gospel. Hence, we shall take this epistle as our guide, but shall refer to the gospel as well. In 1 John it says, "Our fellowship is with the Father and with his Son Jesus Christ" (1:3). In context this means that we achieve community with God through Jesus Christ and, more precisely, through the acceptance of Jesus Christ in faith in accordance with the authorized preachers who testify to him and proclaim him. "Life was made manifest and we saw it and testify to it, and proclaim to you the eternal life which was with the Father and was made manifest to us," the author remarks in the second verse. First, we intend to clarify the distinctive character of the Johannine notion of community with God and then compare it with others of his day.

I   THE JOHANNINE NOTION IN ITS
CHARACTERISTIC FEATURES

As every religious attitude toward life, John's preaching is based on the conviction that human existence is realized only when it attains its goal in absolute being, in God. The question, however, that concerns all religions is how this goal is to be reached. The Christian answer is clear: God himself has willed to establish this living union with us, to draw us into his fellowship by sending us his Son and through him making it possible for us to be united with himself. Jesus Christ is the Mediator of salvation, who has given us eternal life in God. Or, we could also say that he has elevated our existence so as to share in the absolute imperishable existence of God. But before we examine this central thought in the Johannine writings, we might focus our attention on his various modes of expression for community with God.

1. This trend of thought is paraphrased in the great epistle by the following expressions: "to be in God" (2:5, 5:20) or "to abide in God" (2:6, 24, 4:13, 15, 16). This union, together with the typical expression "to abide" (μένειν ἐν), is mostly extended (except in 2:6, 24) to the bilateral (reciprocal) formulation "we (abide) in God and God in us." We also meet it conversely, "God abides in us and his love is perfected in us" (4:12). Thus henceforth we may also include in our field of vision those expressions denoting other values abiding in us that are closely related to God, such as "truth" (1:8, 2:4), his "word" (1:10, 2:14), his "anointing" (2:27), his "seed" (3:9), "everlasting life" (3:15), and "love" (4:12). God abides and acts in us by means of everything that comes from him and flows upon us, his word and his truth, his spirit and his life, or again that which embraces everything—his love. He also uses the expression "to have God" (2:23, 5:12), which

also bespeaks the perfect fulfillment of man's search for happiness and union with God, and whose usage can be ascertained in other writings of that time.[3] Whoever possesses God, possesses everything. Finally, the "knowledge of God" again leads to the same result, since "to know God," biblically understood, is simply more than a theoretical knowledge of his existence, for it also means a living union with God and a practical acknowledgment of him.[4] Particularly in the perfect tense ("to have known God," 2:3, 13, 14) does it have the same sense as "to have God" or "community with God."

This brings us to yet another characteristic mode of expression in John's gospel. From Christ's basic priestly prayer we quote: "Now this is everlasting life that they may know thee the only true God and him whom thou hath sent, Jesus Christ" (Jn 17:3). It is not rational knowledge of God that is implied here; nor should "everlasting life" be restricted to such knowledge. On the contrary, in the fourth gospel Jesus denies that the unbelieving Jews know God (7:28, 8:55) and reproaches them, "But I know that you have not the love of God within you" (5:42). True "knowledge

[3] H. Hanse, "Gott haben" in der Antike und im frühen Christentum (Berlin, 1939) and "ἔχω etc.," ThWNT 2 (1935) 822ff.

[4] Cf. J. Hänel, Das Erkennen Gottes bei den Schriftpropheten (Stuttgart, 1923); R. Bultmann, "γινώσκω etc.," ThWNT 1 (1933) 688-719; E. Prucker, Γνῶσις θεοῦ (Würzburg, 1937); G. J. Botterweck, "Gott erkennen" im Sprachgebrauch des Alten Testaments (Bonn, 1951); M. Féret, Connaissance biblique de Dieu (Paris, 1955); I. de la Potterie, "Οἶδα et γινώσκω. Les deux modes de la connaissance dans le quatriéme évangile," Bib 40 (1959) 709-725; R. Schnackenburg, Die Johannesbriefe, exc. 3, p. 95-100.

of God" consists of the union of our life with God—
preserving and unfolding the love of God within us.
Conversely, "everlasting life" is defined as a fellowship that brings "knowledge of God." From this we
realize that the central thought of Johannine theology,
namely, "everlasting [divine] life" signifies nothing
more than the profound and perfect union with God, a
sharing in his life. We can have "life" and have it
"abundantly" (Jn 10:10), only if God himself draws
us into the sphere of his life. From the concept of
"life"[5] stem even further bonds of union, for example,
our being "children of God," for we become that since
we are "begotten by God" (Jn 1:13; 1 Jn 2:29, 3:9, 4:7,
5:1, 4, 18). To be a "child of God" is not simply a
beautiful expression, a mark of honor, but a real,
established, new relationship to God that is granted to
us by his love (cf. 1 Jn 3:1f.). It is by the spirit of God,
by his creative power of life, that we are begotten as
"children of God" (Jn. 3:5f.).

2. By noting John's various forms for expressing the
same thought, we become aware of the emphasis on
community with God. If we take another look at the
particular characteristics of the Johannine notion of
community with God, we might briefly summarize
them in a few points.

a. The Christian's community with God is an intimate,

[5] F. Mussner, ZΩH. *Die Anschauung vom "Leben" im 4. Evangelium* (München, 1952); J. Dupont, *Essais sur la Christologie
de. s. Jean* (Bruges, 1951) 109-149; Ph. Seidensticker, "Frucht des
Lebens. Die sittlichen Wirkungen des Lebens nach Johannes,"
Studium Bibl. Francisc. 6 (Jerusalem, 1955, 1956) 5-84; M. Tur-
ner, "Believing and Everlasting Life, A Johannine Enquiry," *Expository Times* 64 (1952, 1953) 50-52.

bilateral relationship (see below, the reciprocal formula) and not simply a relationship of protection on the part of God, that is, a juridical or moral relationship, but an entering into the life of God, a real founding of man's existence in God, and an implanting of God's life in man—a deep personal relationship and fellowship.

b. Thus, community with God can be represented as a mutual penetration—an abiding of divine being and life in man and God's sharing in man's being and life. However, the personality of God and that of man remain intact. Man is not "mystically" absorbed into God; nor do "the Father" or "the Son" lose their sovereignty. There remains nevertheless a profound personal relationship, whose degree of intimacy could never be found between human persons.

c. Community with God is no fleeting affair, no temporally limited (mystical-ecstatic) experience, but by its very nature remains a continuing possession, a salvific good, a constant union that is real and personal. It cannot be striven for by human endeavor or reached by ecstasy. It is not an experience of religious sentiment, but a gift from God that we obtain by faith.

d. Next to faith, which is the fundamental attitude on the part of man, the sacraments play an important role as a means to salvation. Baptism brings the "generation from above" (Jn 3:3) or "from God" (1:13; 1 Jn *passim*) and thus establishes the fellowship granted to man by God. Eucharist is the proper sacrament of unity whereby eating the flesh and drinking the blood of Christ unites us most intimately with Christ and through him with God. Here in particular the formulas reflecting the immanent character of this union converge. Jesus says, "He who eats my flesh and drinks my blood abides in me and I [abide] in him" (Jn 6:56). But continuing community of life with him leads also to the sphere of God's own life, preserves and confirms those who believe in their union of life with God (cf. Jn 6:57). The unity of Jesus with his Father is the ideal, the analogy, and the basis of community with God that is granted to men (cf. Jn 17:21f.).

e. Community with God is also realized in the life and conduct of the Christian and becomes recognizable in the external manifestation of life—especially in love stemming from God do we recognize those who are united to God and who are "children of God" (cf. 1 Jn 3:18f., 4:16). This love, moreover, is manifested externally in the love of our brothers (cf. 1 Jn 2:10, 3:14, 4:19f., etc.). Thus, community with God establishes a new being and behavior and is easily detected in a man's new relationship to existence, a new self-understanding.

f. The Christian's community with God finds on earth a preliminary but not yet perfect fulfillment. We must keep in mind that we are as yet in the "world," and consequently exposed to the clutches of evil, thus ever in the line of combat (cf. Jn 16:33; 1 Jn 4:4f., 5:4). Perfect community with God will be possible only when we "shall see him as he is" (I Jn 3:2), and that will first be possible in the state of glory (δόξα), when we shall be united with the glorified Christ (cf. Jn 17:24). This true perfection is a new step in our relationship to God, for now we are merely "children of God" and then we shall become entirely similar to him ("like to

him," 1 Jn 3:2)—an ancient expression for ultra nearness to God (cf. Gen 3:5). Until then our community
with God remains grounded in faith, which gives us
hope (1 Jn 3:3) toward such fulfillment.

g. But the most important aspect is what might be
called the "Christological principle." The way to community with the Father is only through the Son. This
Christological and soteriological principle is the
nucleus of Johannine theology. Jesus, in his answer to
Philip, expresses it most concisely and forcefully, "He
who sees me sees also the Father. How can you say:
Show us the Father? Do you not believe that I am in
the Father and the Father in me?" (Jn 14:9f.). Jesus
himself lives in the closest unity with his Father; here
too the reciprocal formula is valid ("I in the Father and
the Father in me"). This concise expression comprises
a profound statement: the Son is completely one with
the Father in will and deed (5:19, 8:29, 11:41f.,
12:49f.), in thought and love (3:35, 10:18, 14:31,
17:24, 26), and finally in nature (cf. 1:1, 5:26, 6:57,
10:30, 17:11, 21). He lives and acts only out of his
unity with the Father, who loved him before the creation of the world (17:24) and whose love he repays in
doing what the Father commands him (14:31). The
mission from his Father to come into the world has no
other purpose than to bring men back to life in God
which they have lost (3:16f.). Since the Father loves
the Son and has given all things into his hand (3:35)
and since he has given him power over all flesh (17:2),
the Son is authorized to grant divine life to all who
believe. As the Father has life in himself and has
granted the Son likewise to have life in himself (5:26),

so too does everyone who believes in the Son receive life from the Son (3:15, 16, 36, etc.). For he is admitted into the sphere of divine life—has "passed from death to life" (5:24). When Jesus promises the Holy Eucharist, he remarks tersely: "As the living Father sent me and I live because of the Father, so he who eats me will live because of me" (6:57). Thus, Jesus Christ, the divine Incarnate Logos, is in person the Word of God who proclaims God's love to us and brings it to us by drawing us into the sphere of divine life and into the closest community with God. Therefore, Christ is the "door" to the life-giving pasture (cf. 10:9f.), and he is the "way" to the Father because he conveys the truth and the life (cf. 14:6).

All these central thoughts support John's message that they who believe in Jesus Christ have attained community with God. For this reason, then, the common expression of "community with God" assumes a different meaning in the mind of this great theologian from that of all other religions and religious groups existing at that time. By studying more closely the comparable modes of speech and forms of expression that represent the spiritual environment of early Christianity, we shall gain even keener insights into the originality of the Johannine notion of community with God.

II THE JOHANNINE NOTION OF COMMUNITY WITH GOD IN COMPARISON TO THE RELIGIOUS ENVIRONMENT

At that time religious searching was quite widespread; spiritual contacts and exchange of ideas were lively, so that we speak of a "syncretism"; and many ideas coming from the outside also influenced Christianity. But we must distinguish these currents and influences by considering them separately.

1. Judaism

Jewish piety in itself was better suited to stress the eminence and transcendence of God; but here, too, though it experienced the nearness of God, it offers few possibilities of contact with John's mode of expression. In Jewish history the notion of the covenant occupies the center—and thus the community of the whole people of Israel with God: "I will be your God and you shall be my people" (Lev 26:11f.). And that too—after the breakdown of the covenant relationship because of unfaithfulness and defection, at least according to God's judgment—is once again the great promise of the messianic era (Jer 7:23, 11:4, 30:22; Ez 11:20, 36:28, 37:27; Zach 8:8). This nearness to God is not merely a moral relationship. Owing to the temple, it is understood as God's dwelling in the midst of his people (Lev 26:11; 3 Kg 8:13; Ez 37:27, cf. 40f.; Zach 2:14f.). The expression "God with us" (Is 7:14, 8:8; cf. Ap 2:3) is characteristic; the Messiah will be so called (Is 7, 14) inasmuch as he is the earthly representative of the heavenly God and king, and is the governor of his kingdom. But this "God *with* us" is not yet the "God *in* us" as in the Johannine signification. Judaism rightly stood reserved and opposed to a mystical piety, even if Jewish mysticism did develop more strongly in individual circles after the destruction of the temple—as we are seeing it more clearly today.[6] In general, Judaism was stronger when it was governed by the fulfillment of the works of the law and by the notions of sin, repentance, and atonement. Only in Jewish Hellenism was there an inclination toward the thought of a union of the soul with God—as can be studied in the case of Philo of Alexandria—but this mystical stream was clearly influenced by Platonic and other Hellenistic thoughts.[7]

The disposition of the pious men of *Qumran* is informative, especially as they appear in the "hymns of praise" (Hodajoth). The one praying is filled with a grateful joy for the "knowledge" granted him by God for the revelation of his "mysteries," for the "elevation" into the community of the "Sons of God" (i.e., the angels), but this is understood differently than in the mystic cults and Gnosticism. The "chosen one" always remains conscious of his great distance from God and remembers that he is a "creature of clay," a "worm" and a sinner (1 QH 1:21f., 3:24, 4:29f., 6:34, 11:12, etc.). He praises God for "having drawn [him] up to

[6] Cf. H. Odeberg, *The Fourth Gospel*, vol. 1 (Uppsala, Stockholm, 1929) *and 3 Enoch or The Hebrew Book of Enoch* (Cambridge, 1928); G. G. Scholem, *Major Trends in Jewish Mysticism* (New York, 1954) and *Jewish Gnosticism, Merkabah Mysticism and Talmudic Tradition* (New York, 1960); H. J. Schoeps, *Urgemeinde, Judenchristentum, Gnosis* (Tübingen, 1956); K. Schubert, "Problem und Wesen der jüdischen Gnosis," *Kairos* 3 (1961) 2-15; J. Maier, *Vom Kultus zur Gnosis I: Bundeslade, Gottesthron and Merkaba* (Talsburg, 1964).

[7] Cf. E. R. Goodenough, *By Light, Light, The Mystic Gospel of Hellenistic Judaism* (New Haven, London, 1935); W. Völker, *Fortschritt und Vollendung bei Philo von Alexandrien* (Leipzig, 1938) 1-47; H. A. Wolfson, *Philo,* vol. 1   rev. ed. (Cambridge, Mass., 1948) 3-86.

an eternal height" and for "having cleansed [him] from numerous transgressions to place [himself] into the ranks of the multitude of the holy ones and to enter into fellowship with the community of the Sons of Heaven" (3:20-22). However, this is no more than a union with the heavenly multitude and a hope for a perfect union with them. The relationship to God himself remains determined by the true fulfillment of the law and by God's protective loyalty to his chosen ones. "They who according to your pleasure will stand before you forever and they who walk the path of your heart will be established for ever" (4:21f.). That reminds us of 1 John 2:17, "He who does the will of God abides for ever." But for such formulations as "He who abides in love abides in God and God abides in him" (4:16), there is no link with the Qumran texts. A more profound community with God, a union with him, is not discernible. This piety retains essentially the stamp of the Old Testament.

2. Pagan Hellenism

Religiously inclined philosophy, namely, Stoicism, by its expressions that at first sound so familiar to the Christian ear, means something entirely different from community with God according to John. The New Testament itself offers in the Apostle Paul's discourse on the Areopagus an example of similarity in terminology (Acts 17:28). Both the first part, "In him we live and move and have our being," as well as the second part, "We are indeed his offspring"—an explicit citation from the Hymn to Zeus by Cleanthes—

breathe the spirit of the then currently popular Stoic philosophy. It addresses God as the Father of men and the deities, speaks of the "kinship" (συγγένεια) of man with God, and draws its ethical demands from this. The lecture of Epictetus ("What is the result of this that God is the Father of men?") is instructive in this regard.[8] He first introduces an old Stoic maxim: "We have all primarily come into existence because of God and God is the Father of men and of the deities." He then develops that this common element between men and God consists in the reason and the will. Finally, he deplores the fact that only a few are conscious of this dignity and take advantage of this kinship with God in accord with their notions. The more deeply founded Stoic teaching of the "seminal reasons" that have fallen upon men from the divine "world reason"—although it loses importance in the popular representation—reveals the complete contrast between this fundamentally pantheistic philosophy and the Christian concept of God. Thereby the Stoic "community with God" is simply a purely natural similarity and kinship with God, even less than that according to Christian standards since the concept of a personal God is lacking. There is no bridge to the Johannine notion of community with God which is entirely intimate, personal, and founded on the common possession of life.

We can ask further how the Johannine notion of community with God is related to the Greek piety of enthusiasm, since the expression "enthusiasm" probably comes etymologically and conceptually from be-

[8] Diss. I, 3 (Ed. Loeb: W. A. Oldfather I, 24ff).

ing "in God" ($\dot{\epsilon}v$-$\theta\epsilon\tilde{\omega}$). According to the latest research
the religion of Dionysius reaches far back and had at
an early time brought the Greek soul under its con-
trol.[9] Compared to the gods of Olympus this religion,
with its elements of the ecstatic, created an entirely
different religious atmosphere—a bewitched world in
which, through the notion of enthusiasm, a "holy in-
sanity" ruled. Nothing could be more opposed to this
emotional piety that lost itself in the drunkenness of
the "fullness of God" than the Johannine piety
founded on faith, a piety that is clear, ethically bal-
anced, and yet warmed by love. So sublime does John
consider this community with God—whose peak and
goal he discerns to be in the future beholding of God—
that he never, not even once, hintingly describes
mystical experiences as visions and ecstasies. He explicitly rejects a corporal view of God upon earth (cf.
Jn 1:18, 5:37, 6:46; 1 Jn 4:12, 20). Man comes to community with God only through faith, not through
ecstasy; and it is a constant experience of salvation, not
a transient sacred frenzy.

3. Gnosticism and Mystery Cults

Other variations of the notion of union with God appear in that vigorous spiritual movement generally
termed "Gnosis." Questions as to how far back it ex-
tends and how much it is related to Christianity con-

[9] Cf. E. Rohde, *Psyche. Seelenkult und Unsterblichkeitslehre der
Griechen* vol. 2, 9-10 ed. (Tübingen, 1925) 11ff.; W. F. Otto,
Dionysos. Mythos und Kultus (Frankfurt a.M., 1933) 87ff.; M.-J.
Lagrange, "Les Mystéres: L'Orphisme" (*Études Bibliques* (Paris,
1937) 82ff.

tinue to be disputed.[10] Since John had to combat early
Gnostic Christological heresies, we can be sure that
some of these notions already existed in his environment. However varied these Gnostic systems might
have been, one basic notion is common to all of them—
man must come to the knowledge of his true nature
or of his "self" and find his salvation by reason of
"Gnosis" ("knowledge"). If he realizes this salvific
knowledge, he will be divinized again and enter into
the heavenly, divine world. Gnostic texts speak frequently about ascending to the world of light and life.
Compared to the striking and deluding appearances of
the cult of Dionysius, the Gnostic notions are more
spiritual and closer to John's terminology and world of
ideas. Nevertheless, the Dionysian expressions are
considerably different. The same is true for the so-
called mystery cults which played a great role in the
Roman-Hellenistic era. They labored toward a "rebirth" and "divinization" of man by mysterious visions
and actions. The boundaries between Gnostic, mystic,
and mysterious notions and expressions are actually
not always clear. But let us consider some significant
texts. A well-known magical papyrus, the so-called
Mithraic Liturgy, describes union with God as a sort

[10] Among recent works see H. Jonas, *Gnosis und spätantiker
Geist*, vol. 1 (Göttingen, 1934 and vol. 2 (Göttingen, 1954); G.
Quispel, *Gnosis als Weltreligion* (Zürich, 1951); E. Haenchen,
"Gab es eine vorchristliche Gnosis?" *Zeitschrift für Theologie
und Kirche* 49 (1952) 316-349; R. McL. Wilson, *The Gnostic
Problem* (London, 1958); R. M. Grant, *Gnosticism and Early
Christianity* (New York, 1959); S. Schulz, "Die Bedeutung neuer
Gnosisfunde," *Theologische Rundschau* 26 (1960) 209-266, 301-
334; H.-M. Schenke, "Hauptprobleme der Gnosis," *Kairos* 7
(1965) 114-123.

of ascension of the soul into heaven, and understands the *unio mystica* that ensues in the world above (ecstatic) as an abiding of God in man. The mystic pleads: "Abide with me in my soul."[11] Except for the notion of being children of God in another passage (6:2, 12), that is perhaps the closest "contact" with John. The differences, however, are unmistakable both linguistically and, even more so, conceptually. In particular, the believing Christian does not need "to step out of himself" by means of any knowledge or vision; nor does he need to rise from this earth into a higher world. He finds community with God in this world by faith alone in the Son of God.

The thirteenth tract of the so-called Hermetic writings deals with the mystery of rebirth. Following Hermes' instructions, his docile pupil, Tat, experiences rebirth by freedom from sense perception and by an ecstatic vision. In a state of perfection, following his divination, he exclaims, "I am in heaven ,upon the earth, in water, in the air . . . everywhere . . . O Father, I see everything and myself in the spirit."[12] That is nothing more than a pantheistic mysticism of divinization. Such a mysticism of union reaches its most forceful expression in many of the magical prayers that speak of such identity: I know you, O Hermes, and you know me. I am you and you are I."[13] John's statements

---

[11] A. Dieterich, *Eine Mithrasliturgie*, 3rd ed. (Leipzig, Berlin, 1923) 14, line 24f.

[12] A. D. Nock and A.-J. Festugière, *Corpus Hermeticum*, vol. 2 (Paris, 1945) tract. 11 and 13, 205f. W. Scott, *Hermetica*, vol. 1 (Oxford, 1924) 246, attempts another reconstruction of the text.

[13] Magical Prayer II, 7, quoted by R. Reitzenstein, *Poimandres* Leipzig, 1904) 20f.

are far removed from all this; they never do away with the boundary between man and God. The person who is raised to the divine sphere of life, who is "begotten by God," never becomes God himself but is only united with him in a real and most intimate way —attaining participation in his life, in his love, in his possessions. He becomes a "child of God" and belongs to the same divine sphere (εἶναι ἐν θεοῦ [1 Jn 3:10, 4:4, 6, 5:19]), but must realize and prove this also in his actions.

The Odes of Solomon[14] show us exactly how mystical and ecstatic piety appears in a garb that is Christian, Gnostic, and syncretic. In order to describe the inner community with God that the soul achieves by its ascent to the "light of truth" (38:1), these hymns employ a plethora of images such as marital love, the "putting on" of the form of the redeemer, God's dwelling in men, the figure of breast-feeding, and so forth. Objectively, it is the redemption through Gnosis that is intended, and the form of the redeemer ("Son," "Christ," or "Lord") is understood in the sense of the Gnostic myth. Everything, however, is clothed in a language that is mystical, visionary, mysterious, and symbolical. Thanks to the Gnosis given by God and to his uniting us with him, an inebriatingly happy knowledge (cf. 11:7f.) and estatic rejoicing (21:6ff.) weave their way through this unusual religious lyric poetry.

---

[14] R. Harris and A. Mingana, *The Odes and Psalms of Salomon*, 2 vols. (Manchester, 1916, 1920); *Die Oden Salomons*, ed. W. Bauer, Kleine Texte 64 (Berlin, 1933). The numbers indicate the Odes and verses.

John himself avoids such images and sensuous descriptions. If we consider the extraordinary experiences of the union with God to be "mysticism," then he is no mystic. For him "community with God" is accessible to all men by faith in Christ. On the other hand, the intimate and mutual union with God in and through Christ, that we experience can perhaps rightly be thought of as a kind of "mysticism," but it nevertheless remains a special and unique one.

Wherever we look we see upon closer examination that John adheres to his characteristic manner of presenting community with God. Through Christ, the Son of God, the believer enters into a community of existence and life with God himself and, at the same time, gains the hope of that yet imperfect union with God (cf. 1 Jn 3:2f.). This final union with God neither can nor should in any way be "anticipated" either by ecstasy, vision, holy rapture, frenzy, or some sort of intensified knowledge. The way is accessible to all in faith provided that they accept God's witness and believe in the Son of God (1 Jn 5:9f.). Union with God is not reserved to individuals, to privileged prophets, mystics, or Gnostics, but rather promises the same thing to everyone and demands the same thing of everyone. Terminologically, perhaps, John does sometimes refer to the Gnosis, but by his appreciation of ethics he holds fast to the best heritage of Judaism. He proclaims the message to his contemporaries and promises them genuine community with God through faith in Christ. John can teach us likewise to proclaim community with God to the men of our day and in the language they understand, for there exists in the depths of modern man—though he may not be aware of it—the longing for God who is true life. Our human existence in the modern world strives toward deeper fulfillment and strains to be merged in the fullness of life—which we call community with God.

CHAPTER IX

Johannine Christology and the Gnostic Myth of the Savior

In the fourth gospel the attentive reader comes upon modes of expression that betray an exceptional degree of reflection upon their formulation. The reader simply cannot ignore such notions as the pre-existence of the "Son" or "Son of Man" and the dualism of an "above" and "below" approached by the movements of "ascending or "descending," respectively. One typical instance is "No one has ever seen God; the only Son who is in the bosom of the Father, he has made him known" (Jn 1:18); another is "No one has ascended into heaven but he who descended from heaven, the Son of Man" (3:13). Is it not possible that these notions and their formulation are mythological, having their roots in Gnosticism, for example? The importance of this question need not be emphasized. Our Christian life is founded on the belief that a historical person, Jesus of Nazareth, is the Redeemer of all men.

As brought out in the preceding chapter it is this Jesus who is the way to union with God. He is the one sent by God to convey revelation and salvation to us. In dealing with these Christological problems we come to grips with the central message of our Christian belief; for if the expressions "descending from heaven" and "ascending" were proved to be bound to a Gnostic myth of a Savior, the very basis of our Christian faith is then questionable. This problem touches the very essence of Christian belief, and we must, therefore, consider seriously all attempts to explain such Christological statements in another way.

R. Bultmann maintains that the Evangelist has appropriated the Gnostic "Myth of the Redeemer" and has used a Gnostic source for Christ's discourses.[1] In this way he seeks to explain the Gnostic-colored language of the fourth gospel. He understands, however, the intention of the Evangelist to place man in an actual situation of decision through the revelation of Christ. All the discourses of Jesus as to who he is and

[1] R. Bultmann, *Das Evangelium des Johannes*, 8th ed. (Göttingen, 1963) 12: "The prologue of John's Gospel, or its source, speaks in the language of Gnostic mythology, and its Λόγος is that intermediary being which is both a cosmological and a soteriological figure, that divine being which has existed from the first beginning with the Father and has become man in order to redeem mankind." Bultmann insists on an older, pre-Christian existence of the Redeemer's myth; although the sources are of a later date, they mingle various names and figures and only allow a hypothetical reconstruction of the alleged uniform myth (p.11f.). For the Gnostic source of Christ's discourses see the book of Bultmann's pupil, H. Becker, *Die Reden des Johannesevangeliums und der Stil der gnostischen Offenbarungsrede* (Göttingen, 1956).

what he does are only a summons, challenging men to decide before God whether they will convert and thus find a new understanding of their existence, or continue to be enslaved by mundane thinking and acting. This is called Bultmann's "existential interpretation," in which the antiquity of the Gnostic myth of the Savior holds an important place. If this view were correct, then the fourth evangelist himself would be an early witness for demythologizing. Thus, all that John reports about Jesus' person, his claims and deeds, as well as what in the foreground seems to be an appraisal of his personal mission and salvific mediation, is merely an external mode of expression meant to lead one to a new and true self-understanding.

In this connection it is not necessary to add that a certain mode of expression, for example, the "ascending and descending" of the Son of Man, is bound to an earlier, antiquated concept of the world that must be brought in line with our contemporary view of reality. However, this spatial category belongs to a religious language employing symbols and imagery, which cannot be completely dispensed with despite our modern, scientific view of the world. Existential theologians hope to go further; they strive to incorporate the person of the Revealer and Redeemer, the historical Jesus of Nazareth, into the process of demythologizing and to deny any personal involvement of his in the redemption. They understand Jesus' appearance and destiny to be only a revelation-event, an "eschatological event," which as such has meaning for every man who comes into contact with its proclamation or "kerygma"). However sincere and respectable this intention may be, we must try to determine the position and intention of the Evangelist himself.[2]

First, we shall consider the existence and the age of the Gnostic myth of the Savior; second, we shall compare it with the Christology of John the Evangelist; and finally, we shall attempt to clarify the historical presuppositions of John's Christological modes of expression.

I   THE GNOSTIC MYTH OF THE SAVIOR

What is the Gnostic myth of the Savior? We must first of all consider the nature of Gnosticism. It is, as R. M. Grant says, "a religion of saving knowledge, and the knowledge is essentially self-knowledge, recognition of the devine element which constitutes the true self. To this recognition is added a bewildering variety of myths and cultic practices."[3] Not a few scholars are

---

[2] For a critique see L. Malevez, *Le message chrétien et le mythe* (Bruges, 1954); J. Macquarrie, *An Existentialist Theology* (London, 1955); R. Marlé, *Bultmann et l'interprétation du Nouveau Testament* (Paris, 1956); G. V. Jones, *Christology and Myth in the New Testament* (London, 1956); A Vögtle, "Rivelazione e Mito," *Problemi e Orientamenti di teologia dogmatica*, vol. 1 (Milan, 1957) 827-960; Th. Müller, *Das Heilsgeschehen im Johannesevangelium* (Zürich, 1961); J. Blank, *Krisis. Untersuchungen zur johanneischen Christologie und Eschatologie*, Freiburg, 1964). Cf. also *Kerygma und Mythos VII: Entmythologisierung und existentiale Interpretation* (Hamburg, Bergstedt, 1963), with various contributions. The following inquiry is a shortened excursus from my commentary on the gospel of John, vol. 1 (Freiburg, 1965) 433-447.

[3] R. M. Grant, *Gnosticism and Early Christianity* (New York, 1965) 10.

of the opinion that the myth of the Savior has an essential significance among these Gnostic myths. Bultmann describes it briefly as follows:

The demonic powers get into their clutches a person who originates in the light-world. . . . The individual selves [the essentially spiritual core of man] of the 'Pneumatics' are none other than the parts or splinters of that light-person. Hence, in their totality they constitute that person—who is frequently called Primal Man—and for whose total redemption they must be released and 'gathered together.' . . . *Redemption* comes from the heavenly world. Once more a light-person sent by the highest god, indeed the son and 'image' [Εἰκών] of the most high, comes down from the light-world bringing *Gnosis*. He 'wakes' the sparks of light who have sunk into sleep or drunkenness and 'reminds' them of their heavenly home. He teaches them concerning their superiority to the world and concerning the attitude they are to adopt toward the world. . . . He teaches them about the heavenly journey they will start at death. . . . And going ahead he prepares the way for them, the way which he, the redeemer himself, must also take to be redeemed. For here on earth he does not appear in divine form, but appears disguised in the garment of earthly beings so as not to be recognized by the demons.[4]

For a long time certain scholars, who were held under the spell of R. Reitzenstein and his theory about the "Iranian mystery of the Redemption" 1921), treated the Gnostic myth of the Savior as though it were an early and unified entity appearing in Gnosticism as the doctrine of "the Redeemed Redeemer," although,

[4] R. Bultmann, *Theologie des Neuen Testaments*, 5th ed. (Tübingen, 1965) 169f.; English ed. *Theology of the New Testament*, vol. 1 (London, 1965) 166f.

of course, under varying forms. It is understandable that New Testament exegetes must rely heavily on the judgments of religious historians, when we consider the difficulties involved in interpreting the old Iranian and later Gnostic literary sources. Thus, there arose the firm conviction of the existence of an ancient "myth of redemption" or "myth of the Savior." According to this interpretation, the "Primal Man" became the "Savior" insofar as he redeemed himself after his fall into matter and returned to the divine realm (the "Ogdoas" or the Plērōma). In this way he co-redeemed (with himself and in himself) men who would be disposed for redemption.

C. Colpe[5] recently described the history of these findings and examined the arguments of this thesis along lines completely in accord with the history of religion. He has shown that the Iranian texts contain a doctrine of redemption that is definitely Gnostic, but that this doctrine also contains notions taken later from either Parsism or Manichaeism. The decisive question concerning the research dealing with Gnosis is whether or not belief in redemption can be traced as far back as ancient Iran. After examining the figure of Gayōmart, whom some have wanted to place at the beginning of the genesis of the Gnostic notions of the primal or primordial man, Colpe concludes:

The comparison between the primordial man in the old Avesta and the Gnostic primordial man could only be made with the help of reconstructions which, on the one hand, are

[5] C. Colpe, *Die religionsgeschichtliche Schule. Darstellung und Kritik ihres Bildes vom gnostischen Erlösermythus* (Göttingen, 1961).

taken from conceptions of the later Pahlavi texts and, on the other hand, from the Gnostic traditions; and thus one could only establish a preliminary step to Gnostic conceptions which perhaps do not really exist in the older Avesta.[6]

Other experts, too, reject the hypothesis that the myth of the Savior originates with Gayōmart. Colpe shows further that it is much the same with regard to the figure of Yima. Neither the "Son of Man" nor the Gnostic Anthrōpos could "be understood as the final terminus of a history that dissolved itself in the Indo-Iranian myth; the intermediate links are wanting."[7] H.-M. Schenke arrives at very similar conclusions: between the myth of the primordial giant, who had been murdered or died, and the doctrine of Manes about the primordial man, we must accept different stages of development, which are, however, not verified.[8]

Using as his point of departure the concept of Manvahmed, G. Widengren has attempted to trace Manichaean notions back to the Zoroastrian religion. In Widengren's own words:

Manvahmed proceeded from the Primal Light, the essence and abode of the Father of Greatness, and that is the reason for its appellation, *ispixt hasēnag*, the original effulgence. Moreover, it is the security and seal of the soul, a guarantee of the salvation of the soul whose higher 'self' it constitutes. The saviour, the Great Manvahmed, clearly stands out as the higher principle in man and, at the same time, as his helper bringing salvation.[9]

[6] *Ibid.* 143.
[7] *Ibid.* 152.
[8] *Der Gott "Mensch" in der Gnosis* (Göttingen, 1962) 19f.
[9] *The Great Vohu Manah and the Apostle of God* (Uppsala-Leipzig, 1945) 18.

He appeals especially to Yasna 49:10: "This, O Maz-
dāh, thou storeth [sic] up in thy house Manah Vohu
and the souls of the righteous ones." Along with H. S.
Nyberg, Widengren interprets this passage to mean,
on the one hand, that Vohu Manah as the heavenly,
cosmic manah resembles the souls that have an individual manah while, on the other hand, Vohu Manah
is a mythical person who is closely bound up with
Ahura Mazda, his father.[10] The presence of Vohu
Manah in the Avesta is so noteworthy that one is
forced to ask whether the (Gnostic) notion of *redemption*, as Widengren cites from the later texts, is already
involved. Along with other scholars, one may suppose
that Manichaeism does employ old Iranian material,
but that of its own accord had first interpreted it
gnostically.

This very difficult question calls for sharper distinctions, both temporally and materially, than was formerly the case. C. Colpe distinguishes three varieties
of the Gnostic doctrine of the redemption which, when
considered together, express the fundamental Gnostic
of "redemption" but differ with regard to "myth of
the Savior": (1) only one prophet, who in varying ways
is called or "sent," is needed to proclaim and reveal the
knowledge that brings redemption; (2) the Gnostic
Savior, in the proper sense, actually descends by way
of the firmament, entering the realm of the "powers"
but not reaching the earth (here too belongs Manvahmed); (3) between both of these types is the Savior
who walks upon the earth in a docetic, unreal body
(particularly in Christian Gnostic systems).[11] In fact,

[10] *Ibid.* 44.
[11] *Die religionsgeschichtliche Schule* 198.

the Hermetic writings and some Christian Gnostic groups do not have a mythological Savior. Likewise, in the "Apocryphon of John," Christ appears only to be a revealer of a mysterious doctrine, a bearer of true knowledge which as such possesses redemptive power.[12]

Thus we may conclude that the whole movement characterized as "Gnosis" depends primarily and principally on the notion of man's redemption by "knowledge," which is a recognition of "self." This movement also traces—not necessarily but preferably—a myth of the Savior symbolizing and illustrating this saving (self-)knowledge. Although Christianity influenced the Gnostic myth of the Savior by way of suggestion and modification, the most important research in this field prohibits us from asserting that the Gnostic myth derives from the Christian message of the Savior. On the other hand, we can hardly maintain that the Gnosis presented Christianity with a ready-made and unified myth of the Savior. It is surely too early to pose the question when and how the Gnostic myth of the Savior or its individual types originated; we merely want to elucidate the difficulty involved in speaking of the Gnostic myth of the Savior as a clearly and definitely outlined reality existing prior to belief in Christ.

[12] For the "Apocryphon of John" see the text-edition of M. Krause and P. Labib, *Die drei Versionen des Apocryphon des Johannes im Koptischen Museum zu Altkairo* (Wiesbaden, 1962); S. Giversen, *Apocryphon Johannis* (Kopenhagen, 1963), with commentary. For an introduction see W. C. van Unnik, *Evangelien aus dem Nilsand* (Frankfurt a.M., 1960); the author remarks: "Jesus here only appears as bearer of true knowledge which is the proper salvific power. In the work of redemption he has no central place. One could delete his appearance totally without changing anything in this book" (p. 90).

II   COMPARISON WITH JOHANNINE CHRISTOLOGY

When we compare John's Christology with the Gnostic myth of redemption, we first notice in his writings the absence of certain aspects that are essential to Gnostic thought. Christ, for example, is not a prototype of man in need of redemption; he is no "primal" or "primordial man" in the sense of either *salvator salvatus* or *salvator salvandus*. Also, the role of a "paradisaic man" and his protological position are nowhere mentioned in John's gospel. Jesus' role as Mediator of creation, which appears only in the hymn to the Logos (Jn 1:3, 10), differs entirely from a cosmogonical explanation of man's nature. Anthropological reflection on the "self" or essence of man, which is somewhat analogous to the speculation on Manvahmed, is also absent. It is a misconception to think, as some scholars have, that the Johannine "Son of Man" collectively includes and represents man in need of salvation.[13]

It cannot be denied that John also discusses man's re-

[13] This opinion was mainly advocated by T. W. Manson and other Anglican scholars; cf. A. J. B. Higgins, "Son of Man-Forschung since 'The Teaching of Jesus,'" *New Testament Essays, Studies in Memory of T. W. Manson*, ed. A. J. B. Higgins (Manchester, 1959) 119-135, especially 126ff. For a critique see O. Moe, "Der Menschensohn und der Urmensch," *Studia Theologica* 14 (1960) 119-129; H. E. Tödt, *Der Menschensohn in der synoptischen Überlieferung* (Gütersloh, 1959) 276-282; A. Vögtle, "Der Einzelne und die Gemeinschaft in der Stufenfolge der Christusoffenbarung," *Sentire Ecclesiam*, Festschrift für H. Rahner (Freiburg, 1961) 50-91, especially 54-65. Cf. also A. J. B. Higgins, *Menschensohn-Studien* (Stuttgart, 1965).

demption and restoration to the world of God. On the contrary, John's Christology is well grounded in and directed toward a soteriological presentation. Nevertheless, John understands the question of redemption in a different way: salvation is the acquittal from God's angry judgment (3:36) and the passage from the sphere of death into the sphere of life (5:24). God requires only one "work," and that is belief in him whom he has sent (6:29). This mission occurred in definite historical circumstances; God's messenger was a historical person, Jesus of Nazareth (cf. 1:17, 45, 17:3, 20:3f.). The question of man's destiny is not answered by reflecting on man's nature, his origin and his goal, or is it made any clearer by using myth. The answer is found in man's returning home to God, the Father of Jesus Christ, by believing in the Son who reveals the Father and paves the way of return for us (cf. 14:2-11).

Thus the Gnostic myth of redemption and Johannine Christology are worlds apart: one is religious philosophy presented in mythic language, the other biblical religion; one is myth, the other history; one is Gnosis, the other faith. Christ's message is completely new; it is not a variation of the Gnostic notion, not a "historization" of myth, wherein the mythic Savior who otherwise appeared on earth (in a figurative mode of expression) has now become "flesh" in the historical person of Jesus Christ. The Christ of John's gospel is always the "Messiah" as well, the Jewish eschatological bearer of salvation—except in a way absolutely surpassing the human hopes of Israel.

We can now limit ourselves to the assertion that John

depends on the Gnostic myth of the Savior only for his modes of thought and expression, without assuming the Gnostic doctrine of redemption. What is the terminological relationship? First of all, concerning the titles of Christ only "Logos" and "Son of Man" would have any claim to Gnostic origin. However, even that cannot be verified as to both titles.[14] It differs very little from the "Son," or "Son of God," or even the "Monogēnes." Gnosticism has much to say about the "Son" and "sons" of certain divine beings and mythical figures. But one can suppose that the fourth evangelist here, as in the case of the "Son of Man," stands in the tradition and development of the Christology of the early Church. We may thus conclude that starting with the titles of Christ it is hardly possible to maintain the Gnostic thesis.

What functions, then, has John predicated of Christ or, better yet, of his "way"? Two modes of expression are characteristic: the "descent and ascent" of the "Son of Man" and the "sending" of the "Son" or his "coming" into the world. Such language is, of course, very frequently employed in the Gnostic texts when they speak of the Gnostic Savior, or at least of the messenger. Mandaean and Manichaean literature, the Odes of Solomon, the Gnostic Acts of the Apostles, and the Gnostic Coptic writings offer abundant material in this respect. The manner of speech cannot (at least not primarily) be traced back to Christianity, but is connected with the Gnostic view of the world, which sharply distinguishes the upper, heavenly world from the lower, earthly world. Thus the "fall" is described

[14] Cf. R. Schnackenburg, *Das Johannesevangelium*, vol. 1 (Freiburg, 1965), exc. 1, 257-269; exc. 5, 411-423.

as a sinking of the higher elements into matter, and the "redemption" is their reinstatement into the Plērōma. The Savior ascends victoriously (through the planetary spheres) and thus shows the way and goal to the "Self" (that is, the divine element in man), which is in need of redemption.

Can John's mode of expression be explained only in terms of this Gnostic-dualistic view of the world? Before we can frame a satisfactory reply, we must first establish that there already exists in the Bible an openness to spatial categories, namely, in the contrasts between "heaven" and "earth," even if both of these realities do not dualistically diverge but are united in the notion of God. Jesus indicates this when he remarks that heaven is the throne of God and the earth his footstool (Mt 5:34f.). In later Judaism, however, the widespread "dualistic" view results in a "heaven" and "earth," an "above" and "below" that are opposed to each other. Jewish thought surely remained true to the historical-horizontal outlook ("this world and that which is to come") without neglecting the spatial-vertical category. The latter category develops especially from the speculation on the "ascent into heaven" of certain men who were carried off to God, in which movement ecstatic visions were striven for (the apocalyptic and mysticism). Rabbinism likewise had not completely cut itself off from such modes of thought and had developed some speculation on the heavenly world. There are many well-known texts that hardly need to be cited here.[15] A noteworthy example comes

15 H. L. Strack and P. Billerbeck, *Kommentar zum Neuen Testament aus Talmud und Midrasch*, vol. 2 (München, 1924), to John 3:12, 31, 424f. and 430f.

from the recently discovered Palestinian Targum, where Joseph of Egypt is censured in a clearly dualistic tone: "He left the grace (or the mercy = ḥsd) from above for the grace from beneath, and the grace which accompanied him from his father's house, and his confidence in the chief butler: he trusted in the flesh, the flesh which passes away and tastes the cup of death."[16] And yet not much is gained from ascertaining such a category of thought; we should examine the problem more closely.

Apocalyptic writing, by its references to the carrying off or "ascensions into heaven" of the great men of antiquity and of biblical history (e.g., Enoch, Moses, Isaiah, Baruch), develops extensively the notion of "ascending." It is possible that John draws upon such speculation when he remarks: "No one has ascended into heaven but he who has descended from heaven, the Son of Man" (3:13). However, the corresponding notion of "descending" is absent in the apocalyptic as well as in Jewish mysticism. "The mystical significance of the καταβασις (i.e., descent) in connexion with preexistence is scarcely traceable," remarks H. Odeberg.[17] Wisdom speculation indicates the very opposite, namely, that wisdom descends to earth. According to the Book of Wisdom, Solomon says: "Therefore I prayed and prudence was given me" (7:7). Later he says: "And passing into holy souls from generation to generation, she produces friends of God and prophets" (7:27). Wisdom's descent from above follows from

---

[16] J. Ramón Díaz, "Palestinian Targum and New Testament," *Nov T* 6 (1963) 75-80, especially 78f.

[17] *The Fourth Gospel,* vol. 1 (Uppsala, Stockholm, 1929) 73.

the fact that she dwells together with God (8:3) and is his companion upon the throne (9:4). "Send her forth from your holy heaven and from your glorious throne dispatch her . . . " (9:10). Still more clearly, in Sirach 24:3-12, wisdom herself describes in mythological language her way from heaven to earth and her dwelling among the people of Israel: "I dwelt in the highest heavens, upon a pillar of clouds stood my throne. I alone compassed the vault of heaven and I wandered through the deep abyss" (v. 4ff.). She finally finds a resting place in Israel (v. 7ff.). Thus, the wisdom literature suggests the notion of the descending of wisdom but does not join it to an ascent that is redemptive.

There are also passages in the Rabbinic literature that closely correlate the notions of "descent" and "ascent." This is true of passages dealing with the Shekinah. According to Aboth de Rabbi Nathan 34, the Shekinah descends to the world ten times and ascends the ten steps, namely, in order to withdraw from the temple. The withdrawal is, however, a penalty. Similar notions are contained in other passages.[18] Therefore, such speculation does not really parallel the descent and the redemption-bearing ascent of the Savior.

This short study indicates that the spatial-vertical category of thought and the individual notions of descending and ascending are verified in Judaism, but that the Johannine notion of the descending and ascending of the Savior is not proven. Thus, the Gnostic myth of the Savior does have value as a paral-

18 Ibid. 90-93; Strack-Billerbeck, *Kommentar*, vol. 3, 172f.

lel. However, we must distinguish between the terminology and the idea intended by the expressions; terminological similarity does not prove conceptual similarity. This conclusion becomes more evident when we reflect upon the designation of the Son as the one sent by the Father into the world. The "sending" of the Redeemer or his "coming" into the world has many parallels in Gnostic literature. In this case, however, we do not have to refer to Gnostic sources for the mode of expression. "Sending" and "coming" are familiar biblical expressions, and the special notion of the sending of the pre-existent Son of God is already found in Paul (Gal 4:4; Rom 8:3). In addition, there are features in John's representation of the "Son" that have no correlative to the Gnostic "messenger." In John's gospel Jesus is depicted as the obedient Son who does only the will of his Father and accomplishes his work (4:34, 6:38), and who freely offers and surrenders his life (10:18, 14:31). Also the office as judge, which Jesus claims as his own (5:22, 27, 30), does not correspond to the representation of the Gnostic messenger. Thus there exists, at the most, certain external terminological agreement, but the Johannine notion itself is completely different. Where, then, are the roots of the Johannine Christological thoughts and expressions to be found?

III   THE PRESUPPOSITIONS OF JOHANNINE
CHRISTOLOGY: A POSITIVE ATTEMPT

If we start with the thesis that John received the Christology of the early Church and developed it in his own way, the motif of descent and ascent does not present anything absolutely new. The hymn to Christ in Philippians 2: 6-11, which in its essentials is certainly pre-Pauline, describes three successive modes of Christ's existence or Christological stages: (1) his existence in the "form of God" (pre-existence: v. 6); (2) his human mode of existence, which involves his taking on the "form of a servant" (v. 7) and his "emptying himself" even to the point of his obedience unto death (v.8); and (3) finally, his glorious cosmic enthronement as ruler, which supposes his presence in heaven once again (v. 9-11). Although these three stages are already defined, as in John, the modes of expression vary. In Philippians we recognize even more clearly the two stages of the "humiliation and elevation" which revert to Jewish conceptions. However, the first stage, that of real (divine-like) pre-existence, far surpasses earlier Jewish notions. Likewise, the notion of "elevation" has not been left without further modification: it is now a "superexaltation" ($\dot{υ}περύψωσεν$ [v. 9]) involving the enthronement of the pre-existent one as ruler of the cosmos—a position he had previously not held according to the hymn's mode of thought. This view, which is bound up with theocratic concepts (enthronement as ruler, divine rule over the world), can scarcely be deduced from Gnostic notions, but does disclose biblical Jewish notions. There is an important link between the older mode of thought in Philippians' hymn to Christ and that of Johannine Christology, namely, the notion of elevation. In John 3:14 "elevation" follows directly upon the reference to the "ascent" of the Son of Man. Thus, John concludes that the "ascent" occurs in the manner of the "elevation," and this notion employed by the Evangelist is part of the genuine, early Christian heritage. John, of course, has interpreted and stamped this thought with his originality inasmuch as he sees the "elevation" of Jesus symbolized and principally accomplished even now on the cross (cf. 3:14). John does so, however, by developing concepts already unmistakably present in the early Christian Church. If the "ascent" of the Son of Man (3:13) means no more than his "elevation" (3:14), it thus suggests that John merely developed a manner of speaking that was already used in the early Church.

Corroboration of this opinion is found in John 20:17, where the risen Lord speaks only of "ascending"; the corresponding "descending" is lacking, and certainly not accidentally or simply determined by the situation, but as essentially connected with the resurrection-proclamation. The oldest resurrection narratives in general mention nothing about the "taking" of Jesus into heaven (cf. however Acts 3:21). This notion must have been interpolated when Jesus was thought of as sitting at God's right hand (cf. Mt 28:18; Acts 2:34ff.). From this Luke develops the notion of the "bodily ascension" of Jesus, expressing it by the term "to be taken up" (ἀναλαμβάνεσθαι [Acts 1:2, 11, 22; cf. Lk 9:51]), once, however, employing the verb "to ascend" (ἀναβαίνειν [Acts 2:34]). John uses neither Luke's realistic and graphic manner of representation nor his linear temporal view, which analyzes the post-paschal event in temporal phases, but he does share the essentially theological notion of "going to the Father" (Jn

13:1, 14:28, 16:5, 28, 17:11, 13) and even uses the term "to ascend."

A comparison of John's mode of expression with other early Christian sources helps us to understand better the meaning of John's notion of "ascending," as well as those influences that assisted him in formulating this notion. Thus, whereas another early Christian hymn to Christ speaks of Jesus' being "taken up in glory" (1 Tim 3:16) and Luke mentions that Christ must "enter into his glory" (Lk 24:26), John expresses this same thought by referring to the "glorification" of Jesus (7:39, 12:23, 13:31f., 17:1, 5). We may thus conclude that the complexus of notions for the paschal or post-paschal event of the enthronement of Christ in heaven contributed to the Johannine mode of writing about the "ascension."

John does not speak of a "superexaltation" of Christ, but rather understands the "glorification" of Christ more as a regaining of that glory he possessed with the Father before the existence and foundation of the world (Jn 17:5, 24). Nevertheless, that notion is not wanting which speaks of the one glorified by the Father now exercising dominion in a way that did not yet belong to him in his pre-existence. It does, however, attain a new Christological formulation: after being glorified by the Father, the Son in his turn should glorify the Father inasmuch as he imparts eternal life to those who believe (Jn 17:1f.). Theoretically, by saying that John was influenced by the conceptual scheme of the "descending and ascending," we could explain the fact that he draws a very close parallel between the pre-existence of Christ and his glorified state. But is not the opposite procedure also plausible? Is it not possible that the Christological view of Jesus' regaining his earlier glory might have led John to the correlation of "descending and ascending"? The Evangelist's real point of view is Jesus' "exaltation" and his dispensing of divine life to all men (cf. 12:32). This places the chief emphasis of Christ's way upon its termination, and it is from this point that the Evangelist contemplates: "What then if you were to see the Son of Man ascending where he was before?" (6:62). Here John reflects on the notion of pre-existence, because it alone completely explains the dignity and grandeur, the power and authority, of this unique eschatological bearer of revelation and salvation.[19] The foundation of Johannine Christology is not some fixed mythological speculation about a Savior who descends from heaven and ascends to it again. Wishing to firmly establish the fact of redemptive power of the Christian Savior, Johannine Christology—as the Christology of the earlier hymn in Philippians (2)—was drawn to lay greater emphasis on Christ's pre-existence. Thus, Christ's way clearly begins "above" and is directed to his return.

Confirmation of this interpretation is found in the discourse on the "bread of life" (Jn 6), in which the theme of the "descent from heaven" and of "ascending" into the heavenly world is developed extensively. Why is "For the bread of God is that which comes down from heaven and gives life to the world" (v. 33, cf. v. 41, 42, 50, 51, 58) stated so emphatically? Because it is a matter of salvation, and because it must be shown that up until this moment divine, enduring, and imperishable

[19] Cf. R. Schnackenburg, *Johannesevangelium*, Exc. 2, 290-302.

life had not been given to men, not even to the Israel-
ites by the manna which they received as a "heavenly"
gift through Moses' intercession while they wandered
in the desert. He must come who was truly in heaven,
who has "descended," and who is by his nature fully
efficacious only when he has once again "ascended"
(6:62). He alone can impart God's spirit and life who
stands above all earthly realities and who is endowed
with God's unlimited power and the abundance of the
spirit. The statement about Jesus' origin and the notion
of "descent" must be considered in the context of the
interests of the early Church and in such a way that
the consideration does not deny the connection with
Jewish presuppositions, even with midrashic traditions.[20]

Moreover, just as the notion of "descent," as we noted
above, was conditioned by Jewish wisdom speculation,
so too is this speculation the most important source
for the notion of pre-existence as applied to Christ in
John's prologue (1:1-3, cf. v. 15). This same complexus
of notions probably influenced John's sermon on the
"bread of life" (6), since "wisdom" also invites men to
fill themselves with her fruits (Sir 24:19, 21, 51:24) by
eating her bread and drinking her wine (Prov 9:1-6).
Thus, the lines converge: in the prologue, the Logos
possesses real pre-existence and, like wisdom, is operative in creation and dwells among men. According to
the sermon on the "bread of life," the true bread of
life descends from heaven; Jesus, in a way similar to

[20] Cf. P. Borgen, *Bread from Heaven* (Leiden, Netherlands,
1965). The influence of midrashic methods, patterns, and terminology upon the discourse of John 6 is the main thesis of this
book.

wisdom, invites us to come to him that we might no longer hunger; he summons us to believe in him that we might no longer thirst (Jn 6:35). Is it not possible that this notion taken from the wisdom speculation may have inspired John's manner of speaking about "descending"? He surely relates the "descending and ascending" with the "Son of Man" (3:13, cf. 6:62). In his Christology, however, the various aspects and points of departure merge into one unified concept: next to the idea of the "Son of Man" stand the notions of the "Son" who is sent by the Father and who returns to him, and that of the Wisdom-Logos who was by God and pitched his tent among men. The final amalgamation of varying elements may and must be credited to the Evangelist.

The fact of a terminological and categorical similarity to the Gnostic myth of the Savior continues to exist. We can, therefore, accept the conclusion that the fourth evangelist, in wanting to bring the Christian message into his Hellenistic environment, took this milieu into consideration in his manner of speaking. He in no way, however, adopted the Gnostic idea itself, but developed his own Christological thoughts from Jewish and early Christian presuppositions. Even if it were an assimilation of the Gnostic myth of the Savior, Johannine Christology would still not have its roots and source in it. If the Evangelist were exposed to the Gnostic posing of the question, he would still have given an entirely different, genuinely Christian reply.

CHAPTER X

The Meaning and Significance
of the Apocalypse

The Apocalypse of John, the last book of the New Testament, is held to be the darkest and most difficult book of the Bible. This book, as all other writings of the New Testament, was presented to the whole Church but was more precisely intended for the community in Asia Minor around the turn of the first Christian century. It discloses the contents of its révelation to all believers in Christ. What makes it so difficult for men of the mid-twentieth century to comprehend is not its prophecy as such, but the guise in which it appears. The Apocalypse stands out as a stranger among the familiar forms of the gospels, the Acts of the Apostles, and the Pauline and other epistles. Unpretentiously, yet impressively, it occupies the last place in the New Testament canon, and for this it had to struggle a long time in the East. To the expert of apocalyptic and apocryphal literature, however, it is by no means an oddity, but has many colleagues in its genus, the so-called apocalyptic literature.[1]

Here, however, we do not want to occupy ourselves with scholarly literary questions, but will attempt insofar as it is possible within the limits of an essay, to scan the contents of this mysterious book. Looking into the Apocalypse may be easier than we perhaps think, since at the very beginning the author explains the meaning and significance of his work: "The revelation of Jesus Christ, which God gave him to show to his servants what must soon take place; and he made it known by sending his angel to his servant John, who bore witness to the word of God and to the testimony of Jesus Christ, even to all that he saw. Blessed is he who reads aloud the words of the prophecy, and blessed are those who hear, and who keep what is written therein; for the time is near" (1:1-3). By explaining several points from these opening words, and thereby allowing the book to speak for itself as much as pos-

[1] Selected bibliography: P. Volz, *Die Eschatologie der jüdischen Gemeinde im neutestamentlichen Zeitalter* (Tübingen, 1934); S. B. Frost, *Old Testament Apocalyptic, Its Origin and Growth* (London, 1952); J. Bloch, *On the Apocalyptic in Judaism* (Philadelphia, 1952); H. H. Rowley, The Relevance of Apocalyptic, rev. ed. (New York, 1964); D. Rössler, *Gesetz und Geschichte in der spätjüdischen Apokalyptik* (Neukirchen, 1959); O. Plöger, *Theokratie und Eschatologie* (Neukirchen, 1959); C. F. Pfeiffer, *Between the Testaments* (Grand Rapids, 1959); G. E. Ladd, "The Revelation and Jewish Apocalyptic" *Evang. Quarterly* 29 (1957) 94-100; B. Vawter, "Apocalyptic, Its Relation to Prophecy," *CBQ,* 22 (1960) 33-46; K. Schubert, "Die Entwicklung der eschatologischen Naherwartung im Frühjudentum," *Vom Messias zum Christus* (Wien, 1964) 1-54; D. S. Russell, *The Method and Message of Jewish Apocalyptic* (London, 1964). For the whole article see the report of research: A. Feuillet, *L'Apocalypse* (Paris, Bruges, 1963), with bibliography.

sible, we shall proceed as best we can to interpret the meaning and significance of the Apocalypse.

I THE REVELATION OF JESUS CHRIST

What the prophet John wants to impart to us is not the disclosure of his own knowledge or of subjective visions, but rather the revelation given him by Jesus Christ, so that he might pass it on to his communities. Indeed, the Jewish apocalyptic writers likewise desire only to transmit divine revelation—at least, this is what they maintain—for example, the author of the pre-Christian Book of Enoch: "The eyes of Enoch have been opened and thus he saw the appearance of the holy one in heaven. The angels allowed me to look at him and I learned from them all that I saw, not for this generation, but for a future one. I will speak about the chosen ones and I will begin my symbolic discourse with them . . ." (Ethiopian En 1:2f.). There do exist, however, significant differences in comparison to such apocalyptic literature.

1. First of all, John's Apocalypse is not an anonymous work; its author gives his name and reveals the circumstances to which he was subjected: "I John, your brother, who share with you in Jesus the tribulation and the kingdom and the patient endurance, was on the island called Patmos on account of the word of God and the testimony of Jesus. I was in the Spirit on the Lord's day, and I heard behind me a loud voice like a trumpet saying: Write what you see in a book and send it to the seven churches, to Ephesus and to Smyrna and to Pergamum and to Thyatira and to Sar-

dis and to Philadelphia and to Laodicea" (1:9-11). Other Jewish apocalyptic writers hide themselves behind the old men of God, behind an Enoch, who was carried off into heaven; an Abraham; a Moses; behind Baruch the prophet or Ezra the scribe. And we know that their books were intended for esoteric groups, for men who considered themselves to be chosen ones who were saved, enlightened ones who understood their hidden allusions, and men of wisdom who could interpret them (cf. 4 Ezra 14:46f.). John's Apocalypse is almost a public ecclesiastical document, which employs only certain cryptograms—and this because caution in time of persecution required it. Compared to other prophecies about the future, it stands out as a frank, powerful document for the communities of Asia Minor, addressing to them words of praise and censure from the Lord (Ap 2-3), and remarking explicitly at the conclusion: "Do not seal up the words of the prophecy of this book; for the time is at hand" (22:10).

2. Furthermore, the other Jewish apocryphal works are only a combining and compiling of older materials from the prophetic books of the Old Testament, adeptly blended, seasoned with interesting questions, and given new interpretation. For example, 4 Ezra 12:10ff. applies the "fourth kingdom" of Daniel 7:7f. in a new and progressive way. We do not want to deny the religious content of these apocalypses, but we know they do not contain any genuine prophecy. Whoever takes into account the background of John's Apocalypse without allowing himself to be misled by the peculiarities of the environment, will discern a vast

unified view of the Christian future. The authenticity of the experience might be disputed by religious historians, but for the authenticity of its revelation we have an unerring criterion. This granted, we come to that which is most important.

3. Our Johannine Apocalypse aims to give the revelation of *Jesus Christ*; but we know this revelation from the gospels and can verify it by comparing the prophecies of the Apocalypse with them. Does John's Apocalypse contradict or confirm Jesus' words concerning the future? The Synoptics compile a discourse of Jesus' about the final days (Mk 13), which certainly contains everything important, according to the understanding of the early Church, that Jesus had said about the future.[2] A comparison of this miniature, so-called synoptic apocalypse with our present Johannine Apocalypse is extremely useful here. A careful study shows that the Johannine Apocalypse—with the exception of several particular points which even in modern times are not readily understood—prophesies nothing essen-

[2] On Mark 13 see F. Busch, *Zum Verständnis der synoptischen Eschatologie. Markus 13 neu untersucht* (Gütersloh, 1938); G. Harder, "Das eschatologische Geschichtsbild der sog. kleinen Apokalypse Mc 13," *Theologia Viatorum* 4 (1952, 1953) 71-107; G. R. Beasley-Murray, *Jesus and the Future* (London, 1954); *A Commentary on Mark Thirteen* (London, 1957); W. Marxsen, *Der Evangelist Markus* (Göttingen, 1956) 101-140; J. M. Robinson, *Das Geschichtsverständnis des Markus-Evangeliums* (Zürich, 1956) 91-94; E. Grässer, *Das Problem der Parusieverzögerung in den synoptischen Evangelien und in der Apostelgeschichte* (Berlin, 1957) 152-170; J. Schmid, *Das Evangelium nach Markus*, 3rd rev. ed. (Regensburg, 1954) 234-250; Ch. Perrot, "Essai sur le Discours eschatologique," *Recherches des Sciences Rel* 47 (1959) 481-514; H. Conzelmann, "Geschichte und Eschaton nach Mc 13," *ZNW* 50 (1959) 210-221.

tially new when compared with Jesus' great discourse on the parousia and his proclaiming of God's perfect kingdom. In both prophecies we find predictions of persecutions and seductions of the disciples or believing men, the foretelling of disaster and distress, or cosmic catastrophes, and finally of Christ's coming in power and glory. Closer analysis of Jesus' discourse on the final days also reveals that his intention was not to give clues for calculating the end, or to satisfy a devout or irreligious curiosity with regard to the future hidden by God, or to make possible a historical document of the final days or a topography of heaven and hell. No, he intended something totally different, namely, to prepare his disciples for the trials that would come, to inspire them, encourage and console them: Take heed to yourselves! (Mk 13:5, 9). Do not be alarmed! (v. 7). He who endures to the end will be saved (v. 13). Watch! (v. 33, 35, 37).

4. We can check this even further. The very arrangement of the Apocalypse agrees in broad outline with Jesus' discourse on the final days. In Mark 13 we can easily discern these categories: in verses 5-13, beginning of the misfortunes of the final days (wars, famines and other plagues, more persecution of his disciples); in verses 14-23; the "great tribulation" with "the desolating sacrilege" (v. 14), probably the antichrist, and again, false messiahs and prophets (v. 21f.); finally in verses 24-27, cosmic cataclysms which will directly introduce the parousia. At this point the discourse breaks off, but from Jesus' other preaching we know that this is followed by the resurrection and judgment, and that finally God's glorious kingdom will

dawn. To this we compare the design of John's Apocalypse in rough outline: the beginning of the eschatological confusion and suffering (5-11), represented in
the vision of the seven seals and the seven trumpets;
then the great battle of the final days between God
and Satan (12-20). This second part corresponds to
"the great tribulation" in Mark 13. It is introduced by
the well-known vision of the attack of the dragon on
the heavenly woman and her child (Ap 12), figure of
Satan's attack against the church; then, Satan's ac-
complices appear (13): the antichrist (the beast from
the sea) with his deceitful assistant (the beast from the
earth); next the seven bowls of wrath are emptied
(15-16), and at the end Babylon, the capital and representative of Satan's kingdom, is condemned (17-18);
and finally we reach the great triumph of the Messiah,
in which the parousia of Christ is represented (19).
The latter is the magnificent counterpart to the account
of the parousia in Mark 13, but more fully explained
under the image of a great battle between the glorious
"rider on the white horse" and the antichrist, the false
prophet and the "kings of the earth," i.e., the rep-
resentatives of the nations opposed to God: "Then I
saw heaven opened, and behold, a white horse. He who
sat upon it is called faithful and true, and in righteousness he judges and makes war. His eyes are like a flame
of fire, and on his head are many diadems; and he has
a name inscribed which no one knows but himself. He
is clad in a robe dipped in blood, and the name by
which he is called is The Word of God. And the armies
of heaven, arrayed in fine linen, white and pure, followed him on white horses. From his mouth issues a

sharp sword with which to smite the nations, and he will rule them with a rod of iron; he will tread the winepress of the fury of the wrath of God the Almighty. On his robe and on his thigh he has a name inscribed, King of kings and Lord of lords" (19:11-16). What Christian does not understand this imagery? The images that follow are perplexing—those about the kingdom lasting a thousand years and the final assault of the multitude of nations hostile to God—but then we hear about the universal resurrection and judgment (20). Finally, the last part of the Apocalypse describes the very focal point of Jesus' preaching, God's perfect kingdom of the final days, represented by the images of the new heaven and the new earth, of the marriage of the lamb to the virgin church, and of the new city of God, the holy Jerusalem.

Up to this point one thing should be clear: John's Apocalypse is genuine Christian prophecy which only serves to confirm the words and promises of Jesus. It is, as the seer himself says, the revelation of Jesus Christ, and the nucleus of its content agrees with that which we hear from the mouth of Jesus in the gospels.

II PROCLAIMED BY JOHN, WHO TESTIFIES TO WHAT HE HAS SEEN

The Apocalypse is a book of visions. The external style of these visions strongly resembles the Jewish apocalypses. The seer from Patmos also employs older prophetic material, moves about easily among the usual images of writing, uses color and number symbolism, hears mighty voices, horns, and trumpets; he sees frightful apparitions on earth and the magnificent throne of God in heaven, together with the whole heavenly court (see Ap 4). We need not be as concerned with the literal meaning of his words as with the meaning of the visions. To interpret this figurative and symbolic language in its particulars is not always easy; therefore, we shall consider only the actual interests of the prophet. Here, doubtlessly, the *visions of calamities*[3] claim an important place: in them many then currently historical features appear, including horrors which disturbed men of that day. Well known are the four apocalyptic horsemen at the beginning of chapter 6. In the succession of plagues we may search for earthly catastrophes and cosmic cataclysms, but not for a historical lapse of time; the pictures paint in many variations the increasing hardships and the mounting intensity of God's punishment. It would not be correct to interpret a part of these visions as historically verifiable while interpreting the other part as referring to metahistorical, eschatological phenomena concerned with the "end."[4]

That is already indicated in the artificial, but artistic, arrangement. First, the Lamb opens the seven seals of the book that contains God's design, and with the

[3] Cf. G. Bornkamm, "Die Komposition der apokalyptischen Visionen in der Offenbarung Johannis," *ZNW* 36 (1937) 132-149; H. P. Müller, "Die Plagen der Apokalypse. Eine formgeschichtliche Untersuchung," *ibid.* 51 (1960) 268-278.

[4] In such way several Catholic scholars: cf. H. M. Féret, *L'Apocalypse* (Paris, 1946) 297ff.; M.-É. Boismard in *La Bible de Jérusalem* (Paris, 1953) 81; St. Giet, *L'Apocalypse et l'histoire* (Paris, 1957); A. Feuillet, *Études Johanniques* (Paris, 1962) 228-271. There are many modifications, cf. A. Feuillet, *L'Apocalypse* 45-52.

breaking of each seal new events occur as provided by God (5:1-8:1). The vision of the seven trumpets (8:2-11:19) grows out of the vision of the seals; and again new punishments follow the blare of each trumpet. After the blast of the fourth trumpet an eagle cries three mighty "woes" upon those who dwell on the earth (8:13). But with the start of the seventh trumpet (11:15) only two "woes" are completed (cf. 9:12, 11:14). The representation is interrupted by the visions of the woman and the dragon (12) and of the two beasts (13), as well as intermediary scenes (14). Then a final series of seven plagues begins, the emptying of the bowls of wrath. "Then I saw another portent in heaven, great and wonderful, seven angels with seven plagues, which are the last, for with them the wrath of God is ended" (15:1). "Then I heard a loud voice from the temple telling the seven angels: Go and pour out on the earth the seven bowls of the wrath of God" (16:1). They are then emptied upon the continents, upon the sea, upon the rivers, upon the sun, upon the throne of the antichrist, and upon the great Euphrates river, on whose banks his metropolis, Babylon, lies. With this the judgment of "the great harlot" Babylon is introduced (17-18). We may conclude that everything is arranged in such way that there is a chain of continuous, ever increasing plagues and punishments, though interrupted by special portents, intermediary scenes, and anticipatory hymns of victory. This is only a long and impressive representation of the tribulations already effective at the present time and continuing to the end of time and human history.

However, we would thoroughly misunderstand the prophet if we were to consider him intent on spreading anxiety. Into these pictures of horror again and again are blended others that should overcome the anxiety and fear of Christians, glimpses of heaven where the heavenly court in anticipation already praises God's victory. Great peace and confidence flow down from heaven upon the earthly church of martyrs, proven by suffering. Even after the breaking of the first seal, after the exit of the apocalyptic horsemen, it is reported: "When he opened the fifth seal, I saw under the altar the souls of those who had been slain for the word of God and for the witness they had borne; they cried out with a loud voice: O Sovereign Lord, holy and true, how long before thou wilt judge and avenge our blood on those who dwell upon the earth? Then they were each given a white robe and told to rest a little longer, until the number of their fellow-servants and their brethren should be complete, who were to be killed as they themselves had been" (6:9-11). Before the breaking of the seventh seal an intermission appears: Then the 144,000 servants of God are marked with the sign of God, that is, with a sign of protection so that they will be defended in the coming time of affliction (7:1-8). In an anticipatory scene[5] the

[5] The second paragraph (12:9-17), introduced by "after this I looked" does not mean a complementary group to the 144,000 sealed servants of God but a new vision of the whole community at the end. Parallel to this "anticipatory" scene are also 14:1-5 and 15:2-4. Cf. B. Häring, Die Botschaft der Offenbarung des heiligen Johannes (München, 1953) 153-166; A. Wikenhauser, Die Offenbarung des Johannes, 3rd rev. ed. (Regensburg, 1959) 65-70.

prophet beholds those who have come from the great affliction and who have washed their robes in the blood of the Lamb. "Therefore are they before the throne of God, and serve him day and night within his temple; and he who sits upon the throne will shelter them with his presence. They shall hunger no more, neither thirst any more; the sun shall not strike them, nor any scorching heat. For the Lamb in the midst of the throne will be their shepherd, and he will guide them to springs of living water; and God will wipe away every tear from their eyes" (7:14-17). What is different here when compared with the prophecy of consolation that Jesus gave his disciples in his discourse on the final days? "Whoever perseveres to the end will be saved" (Mk 13:13). "Behold, I have told you all things beforehand" (13:23). The meaning of these terrifying pictures is: be prepared for every coming event, plagues and trials; do not waver in faith, but remain constant. God already seizes his power to destroy the powers of evil and establish his kingdom.

Grand hymns of victory again and again ring out during the gruesome events on earth—a heavenly liturgy celebrated by the angels and the twenty-four elders which surely echoes the earthly liturgy of the Christian community.[6] After the last trumpet, but still before the furious assault of the dragon on the woman, we hear in anticipation the hymns of jubilation in

[6] Cf. G. Delling, "Zum gottesdienstlichen Stil der Johannes-Apokalypse," *Nov T*, 3 (1959) 107-137; T. F. Torrance, "Liturgie et Apocalypse," *Verbum Caro* 11 (1957) 28-40; M. H. Shepherd Jr., *The Paschal Liturgy and the Apocalypse* (Richmond, 1960); P. Prigent, *Apocalypse et Liturgie* (Neuchâtel, Paris, 1964).

heaven: "We give thanks to thee, Lord God Almighty, who art and who wast, that thou hast taken thy great power and begun to reign. The nations raged but thy wrath came, and the time for the dead to be judged, for rewarding thy servants . . ." (11:17f.). Then the seer looks toward the overthrow of the dragon who has led the world astray, and he hears a mighty voice in heaven proclaiming: "Now the salvation and the power and the kingdom of our God and the authority of his Christ have come, for the accuser of our brethren has been thrown down . . ." (12:10). After passing judgment on Babylon, the great harlot, even before Christ appears as victor at the parousia, John hears once again something like the voice of a great multitude, the sound of rushing waters and of deafening thunderpeals: "Hallelujah! For the Lord our God the Almighty reigns. Let us rejoice and exult and give him the glory, for the marriage of the Lamb has come, and his Bride has made herself ready . . ." (19:6f.).

What a difference in comparison to the representations of the Jewish apocalyptic writers who often give an impression of weakness and dejection. But here, in the case of our Christian seer, lives a joyful certainty that the victory has already been purchased by the blood of the Lamb and that they who follow him will soon wear the white robes of the victor. They have conquered the dragon "by the blood of the Lamb and by the word of their testimony, for they loved not their lives even unto death" (12:11). John's Apocalypse is not a gloomy book, but one that is uplifting, calming, gladdening.

There remain numerous problems posed by the figurative and symbolical language of the seer (e.g., 11:1-14), which we cannot deal with here. Let us only consider the *events after the parousia* (20-22:5). A much disputed and dominant topic is the announcement of the kingdom that is to last for a thousand years (20:1-6). During this period Satan is bound, so "that he should deceive the nations no more, till the thousand years were ended. After that he must be freed for a little while" (v. 3). It appears as though only a partial resurrection may take place, namely, of the martyrs who will rule with Christ for a thousand years (a symbolical number, of course). This prophecy, which has no parallel in Jesus' words, draws upon images from the books of Ezechiel and Daniel and has given occasion for fanciful movements and expectations. Perhaps it is only an image for the reward of the martyrs who should now reign with Christ because of humiliations they suffered. Other exegetes explain it as a scene that is retrospective, describing the life of the blessed with Christ after Satan's defeat at the crucifixion (cf. 12:9-12). More probably, however, it is only the manner in which the scene is represented, employing different images that have been depicted one after another and which should be seen as essentially one. There occurs a duplication which deserves our attention: the triumph of the Messiah in which the exalted Christ conquers the antichrist and the false prophet, hurling them into the lake of fire (19:19f.), and then the attack of the peoples in which Satan himself is destroyed and likewise cast into hell (20:9f.). In between is the image of the kingdom lasting a thousand years, which serves as a contrast-scene to the punishment of the antichrist and his followers (19:20f.), and thus is an image for the reward of the faithful ones.[7] In any case we can be sure that there is only one bodily resurrection, namely, of all the dead who are judged by what they have done, as it is later depicted (20:11-15).

Everything that comes after the parousia belongs to the future world and is unimaginable for us. To describe this further the prophet is only capable of imagery taken from the former world and its spatio-temporal relationships. All our categories of thought and sense perception, however, fail before the prospect of such a perfect world. Will there still be a before and after, an above and below? But the prophet himself knows no other way to describe the new heaven and the new earth than under the image of a city, of the holy Jerusalem coming down from heaven (21:1f.), and he describes in detail its walls and gates, its dimensions of length and width and height and its center (21:10-22:5). He is, nevertheless, aware of the symbolic and inadequate character of his description: "And the city has no need of sun or moon to shine upon it, for the glory of God is its light, and its lamp is the Lamb. By its light shall the nations walk; and the kings of the earth shall bring their glory into it" (21:23f.). "The throne of God and of the Lamb shall be in it and his servants shall worship him; they shall

[7] In this difficult topic see H. Bietenhard, *Das Tausendjährige Reich*, 2nd ed. (Zürich, 1955); M. Rissi, *Zeit und Geschichte in der Offenbarung des Johannes* (Zürich, 1952) 151-158; A. Gelin, "Millénarisme," *Dict. de la Bible*, Supplém. 5, 1289-1294; R. Schnackenburg, *God's Rule and Kingdom* 339-346; A. Feuillet, *L'Apocalypse* 98-101; H. Schumacher, *Das tausendjährige Königreich Christi auf Erden* (Stuttgart, 1964).

see his face and his name shall be on their foreheads.
. . . The Lord God will be their light and they shall
reign for ever and ever" (22:3-5).

III WHAT MUST SOON TAKE PLACE

The estimation of the time of the events seen by the
prophet is a difficult and disputed problem. He himself
remarks in the introduction: "Soon" and "the time is
near" (1:1, 4), the time, namely, of the fulfillment. He
repeats at the end of the book that the angel should
show the servants of God "what must soon take place"
and the Lord tells the prophet, "Behold, I am coming
soon" (22:6f.); and once again at the very end, "Yes,
I am coming soon," and we only hear the response,
"Amen, let it be so. Come, Lord Jesus" (22:20). John,
therefore, lives in hopeful expectation that Christ will
"soon" appear at the parousia and this is in fact the
basic tenor of the whole prophetical book. Also in his
letter to the community at Philadelphia the Lord permits him to comment on this loyal and trustworthy
community: "Because you have kept my word of patient endurance, I will keep you from the hour of trial
which is coming on the whole earth, to try those who
dwell upon the earth. I am coming soon; hold fast what
you have, so that no one may seize your crown"
(3:10f.).

But how are we to understand the expressions that
the events of the final days are coming "soon,"
"shortly"?

The only satisfying answer, it seems, can and must be
drawn from the fact that the prophet gives us a

prophetic view. In such a view it is not seldom that present and future fuse together; new images are always breaking through, images for the future whose building materials the prophet takes from his time. The author sees in the events of his own time the beginning and dawning of the end, and he paints the future strictly eschatological events in contemporary colors.[8] He cannot recognize the span of time; his perspective is curtailed. Its remoteness draws him to the present, and in the present he grasps the future. All the prophets acted in this way and yet Jesus continues to make use of the prophetic approach. There is no falsehood in this; ultimately it is not a matter of the space of time but a matter of the urgency of time and of the challenge involved for all men. If the things that the seer beholds should one day certainly occur without its exact date being fixed, he may rightly say "soon," "shortly." God's calculation of time is different from ours; there is no temporal dimension for him —only the content of time is important. The events

[8] Therefore, neither a strict interpretation in lines of contemporary history nor a merely eschatological explanation is correct, but one must combine both points of view. To this principal question of interpreting the Apocalypse see A. Wikenhauser, *Einleitung in das Neue Testament*, 4th ed. (Freiburg, 1961) 401-404; American ed. *New Testament Introduction* (New York, 1963). Cf. further L. Goppelt, "Heilsoffenbarung und Geschichte nach der Offenbarung des Johannes," *Theol. Literaturzeitung* 77 (1952), col. 513-522; M. Rissi, *Zeit und Geschichte*; H. Schlier, "Zum Verständnis der Geschichte nach der Offenbarung Johannis," *Die Zeit der Kirche* (Freiburg, 1956) 265-244, and "Jesus Christus und die Geschichte nach der Offenbarung des Johannes," *Besinnung auf das Neue Testament* (Freiburg, 1964) 358-373; M. Hopkins, "The Historical Perspective of Apoc 1-11," *CBQ*, 27 (1965) 42-47; see also references cited above in note 4.

during the final days, however, approach us and challenge us. They can occur at any time and establish us in the moment of decision. They call to us and warn us to be watchful and prepared, to be courageous and confident. That was Jesus' intention in his discourse on the final days—and the same is true of John's intention. That is the genuine eschatological attitude, and the whole of primitive Christianity was carried along by it: constant alertness, a burning longing and yet a calm composure. With this we come to the final point, the significance of the Apocalypse for the reader then and for the Christian now.

IV BLESSED IS HE WHO READS ALOUD AND THOSE WHO HEAR THE WORDS OF HIS PROPHECY

Why are the hearers blessed? Because by hearing it is presupposed that one will come to an inner understanding and from this will form one's attitude in the time of trial. In each letter to the seven communities in Asia Minor there is the admonition: "Whoever has an ear, let him hear what the Spirit says to the churches" (2:7, 11, 17, 29, 3:6, 13, 22). But where does the Spirit, who also speaks in prophecy, wish to lead the Christians? To the very same eschatological virtues of interior alertness, constant patience, and the composed confidence of victory. The summons to vigilance is joined with the image of the thief in the night. John, in Christ's name writes severe words to the community at Sardis: "I know your works; you have the name of being alive, and you are dead. Awake. . . . If you will not awake, I will come like a thief and you will not know at what hour I will come upon you" (3:2f.). The same admonition is given to all, almost unexpectedly, after the sixth bowl of wrath has been emptied and the parousia not too far off: "Behold, I am coming like a thief. Blessed is he who watches and keeps his garments . . ." (16:15).

Thus, the hour of Christ's coming still remains uncertain and, in spite of all that, unawaited. But everything that is to come is in God's plan, if we take serious note of "what *must* soon take place." It is the "must" of divine determination that weaves its way throughout the whole book. God has determined the course of events, has arranged the very hour for all to happen, has cast the lot for the individual Christian. "If anyone is to be taken captive, to captivity he goes; if anyone is to be slain with the sword,[9] with the sword he is slain. Here is the patience and the faith of the saints" (13:10). This marvelous observation expresses the basic challenge to the Christian in the time of evil before the end. "The constant patience and faith of the saints." It is for this reason that confessors and martyrs were esteemed and praised so highly: the attitude in which they conquered the rage of Satan and defied the power of the antichrist, those who "did not worship the beast (the antichrist) and his image and did not accept his mark upon their foreheads or upon their hands"[10] (20:4); they now deserve to reign with Christ. This

[9] For a reading other than the generally accepted one see J. Schmid, "Zur Textkritik der Apokalypse," ZNW, 43 (1950, 1951) 112-128, especially 112-125.

[10] John thinks concretely of those Christians who opposed the impious worship of the emperor. They did not worship the image of the emperor who demanded divine honor.

passive opposition to evil and its intrinsically mundane power, this union with God alone even if it means peril to one's life and even death, is the constancy of the saints.

He who reads aloud hears the voice of the heavenly Lord himself who in the seven letters encouragingly addresses him: "To him who conquers I will grant to eat of the tree of life which is in the paradise of God" (2:7). "He who conquers and who keeps my works until the end, I will give him power over the nations" (2:26). "He who conquers shall be clad thus in white garments and I will not blot his name out of the book of life; I will confess his name before my father and before his angels" (3:5). "He who conquers, I will make him a pillar in the temple of my God" (3:12). "He who conquers I will grant him to sit with me on my throne as I myself conquered and sat down with my Father on his throne" (3:21).[11]

The whole Christian community on earth, however, already hears the hymns of victory sung by the multitude in heaven and can do nothing else but praise God again and again in the thick of their confusion and persecution. "Praise our God, all you his servants, you who fear him, small and great" (19:5). "Great and

[11] With regard to these letters, their structure, and theological meaning see W. M. Ramsay, *The Letters to the Seven Churches of Asia* (1904), new ed. (Grand Rapids, 1963); T. Holtz, *Die Christologie der Apokalypse des Johannes* (Berlin, 1962); R. Schnackenburg, *The Moral Teaching of the New Testament* (New York, 1965) 378-386; H. Zimmermann, "Christus und die Kirche in den Sendschreiben der Apokalypse," *Unio Christianorum*, Festschrift für L. Jaeger (Paderborn, 1962) 176-199; A. Repp, "Ministry and Life in the Seven Churches," *Concordia Theol. Monthly* 35 (1964), 133-147.

wonderful are thy deeds, O Lord God the Almighty.
Just and true are thy ways, O King of the nations. Who
shall not fear and glorify thy name, O Lord? For thou
alone art holy. All nations shall come and worship
thee, for thy judgments have been revealed"
(15:3f.).

What is the Apocalypse? A mysterious book for fanatics and sectarians? A branch of the Jewish apocalyptic, bewildered and muddled? A work bound to its
environment and antiquated? The product of an era
engrossed in mythical and fantastic thought? No! It is
primarily a book of admonition and consolation for the
Christians of Asia Minor around the year 100 A.D.
who had withstood the first assaults of persecution,
who counted the first martyrs among their numbers,
and who had to offer resistance to an omnipotent state
with its impious claims and cruel threats. It is a book
testifying to the faith preserved by the ardor and unbroken strength of the Christian religion; a prophecy
in the spirit of Jesus, which applied his predictions to
the situation at that time and which kept hope alive.
The Apocalypse in this light then is also a book belonging to the whole of Christianity, whatever the century
may be, which can always kindle anew its faith in and
love for Christ, its hope and confidence in God's victory won in the blood of the Lamb.

INDEX